THE BIBLE AND LITERATURE

THE BASICS

D0705552

The Bible and Literature: The Basics provides an interpretive framework for understanding the significance of biblical allusions in literature—even for readers who have little prior knowledge of the Bible. In doing so, it surveys the Bible's influence on a broad range of English, American, and other Anglophone literatures from a variety of historical periods. It also:

- offers a "greatest hits" tour of the Bible
- focuses as much on twentieth- and twenty-first-century literatures as on earlier periods
- addresses the Bible's relevance to contemporary issues in literary criticism such as poststructuralist, postcolonial, feminist, queer, and narrative theories
- includes discussion questions for each chapter and annotated suggestions for further reading

This book explains why readers need a basic knowledge of the Bible in order to understand and appreciate key aspects of Anglophone literary traditions.

Norman W. Jones is Associate Professor of English at The Ohio State University. He has published numerous essays and books about the interplay of religion and literature. His work has appeared in top journals such as *American Literature, Christianity and Literature, Modern Fiction Studies,* and *Studies in American Fiction.*

The Basics

TELEVISION STUDIES
TOBY MILLER

TERRORISM
JAMES LUTZ AND BRENDA LUTZ

THEATRE STUDIES (SECOND EDITION)
ROBERT LEACH

WOMEN'S STUDIES
BONNIE SMITH

WORLD HISTORY
PETER N. STEARNS

THE BIBLE AND LITERATURE

THE BASICS

Norman W. Jones

Dear Charles,

I am grateful for your friendship, our shared scholarly interests, and your vital role in The Guild.

warmly,
Norman

Routledge
Taylor & Francis Group

LONDON AND NEW YORK

First published 2016
by Routledge
2 Park Square, Milton Park, Abingdon, Oxon OX14 4RN

and by Routledge
711 Third Avenue, New York, NY 10017

Routledge is an imprint of the Taylor & Francis Group, an informa business

© 2016 Norman W. Jones

British Library Cataloguing-in-Publication Data
A catalogue record for this book is available from the British Library

Library of Congress Cataloging-in-Publication Data
Names: Jones, Norman W.
Title: The Bible and literature : the basics / Norman W. Jones.
Description: New York : Routledge, 2015. | Includes bibliographical references and
  index.
Identifiers: LCCN 2015021802
Subjects: LCSH: Bible and literature. | Bible as literature. | English
literature. | European literature.
Classification: LCC BN56.B5 J66 2015 | DDC 809/.93522—dc23
LC record available at http://lccn.loc.gov/2015021802

ISBN: 978-0-415-73884-2 (hbk)
ISBN: 978-0-415-73886-6 (pbk)
ISBN: 978-1-315-72713-4 (ebk)

Typeset in Bembo
by Swales & Willis Ltd, Exeter, Devon, UK

CONTENTS

ACKNOWLEDGEMENTS

I am grateful to the many people who helped bring this project to fruition. I should first mention the students in my Bible classes with whom I've been privileged to work over the years: our conversations have helped me to understand the need for a beginner's book such as this one and have also helped me to understand the Bible in new ways. The people at Routledge and their affiliates have been exceptionally supportive—Catherine Hanley, Ruth Hilsdon, Colin Morgan, Siobhán Poole, Iram Satti, and their colleagues. Joe Ashby offered enthusiasm, inspiration, and the opportunity to workshop some of the early material. Anonymous readers provided expert guidance. Cynthia Callahan, Hannibal Hamlin, David Herman, and Karen Winstead gave generously of their time and energy, offering thoughtful and tremendously helpful feedback. Finally, Heidi and Riley patiently shared our home with this project for longer than they might have liked, graciously going above and beyond the call in order to support its Bible-obsessed author. I'm fortunate to be so indebted in all these ways and more.

INTRODUCTION: THE BIBLE AS WITNESS TO THE POWER OF STORIES

What do Harry Potter, Hamlet, and the biblical King David have in common? More than meets the eye. Despite being separated by nearly three thousand years, these figures share powerful connections with each other through the Bible. This chapter explores those connections in order to introduce and illustrate the larger topic of this book: the Bible and literature.

First, however, some clarifications and caveats are in order. This book is for readers who want to learn more about the special relationship between the Christian Bible and imaginative literature—that species of writing concerned less with falsifiable claims about how the world actually is than with fictional possibility, poetic reflection, and wonder. I focus on imaginative literatures written in English, mostly by British and American writers but also by some Anglophone writers from Africa, Australia, the Caribbean, Canada, and India. In order to address a diverse range of literatures while still allowing enough space to provide a comprehensive overview of the Bible, I offer only brief glimpses into many complex works of literature. Please take these glimpses as invitations to read more of these works in their entirety. They are worth it! I hope you will also feel encouraged to do your own reading in the Bible. This book is especially for those who do not know the Bible well or perhaps at all, which is why I devote more attention to it.

That said, I do not aim to introduce the reader to the academic field of biblical studies. Scholars in that field primarily explore the historical contexts and specific contributions of the many authors and editors whose work is collected in the Bible. Such scholars seek to establish the most likely intentions of those authors and editors, also trying to determine what sources they might have used. Imaginative literatures in English were composed centuries if not millennia after any biblical text, so they bear no direct relevance to this kind of research into the origins of the Bible. Yet the methods used by literary scholars—especially the kinds of questions we ask—have influenced biblical studies scholars, which means that even though this book does not survey the field of biblical studies, the methods discussed here can indirectly illuminate one aspect of that field.

A newer aspect of biblical studies bears direct relevance to the topic of this book: reception history, which is the study of how the Bible has been interpreted by groups and individuals in various cultural and historical contexts. If you want to explore references to the biblical story of Cain and Abel—the first murder, according to the Bible—in Shakespeare's play *Hamlet* (c.1600), then twenty-first-century research about the origins of the biblical story will not be very helpful. Instead, you should turn to the work of scholars such as Hannibal Hamlin, which illuminates how the Cain-and-Abel story was likely to have been interpreted in early seventeenth-century England. Such scholarship contributes to the long, complex history

The **reception history** of the Bible is the history of the various ways in which the Bible has been interpreted—not only by theologians but also by everyone else, including artists, politicians, and ordinary people. Philosopher Hans-Georg Gadamer (1900–2002) argued that our own cultural and historical contexts unavoidably inform our interpretations of texts. Reception history developed from that premise. It documents how interpretations of a given text have varied over time.

of how the Bible has been "received." This book introduces you to literary aspects of that reception history.

When it comes to this literary reception history, we need to remain open to learning about many different ways of interpreting the Bible. After all, there are a wide variety of religious and non-religious views represented in the vast number of literary works that have been influenced by the Bible. The authors who penned these works include atheists and agnostics as well as adherents to myriad religious traditions. All such worldviews are thus relevant to the topic at hand, and all are welcome here: I do not presuppose the reader's adherence to any particular religious or secular (non-religious) worldview.

By the time you finish this book, you will:

- be familiar with many of the Bible's most famous themes, symbols, phrases, and stories—its "greatest hits";
- be able to identify clear allusions to these "greatest hits" when you come across such allusions in works of literature;
- understand the larger contexts and patterns of influence for such allusions, which will help you explore their significance when you encounter them on your own;
- be able to use the resources in this book to guide further reading of relevant scholarship, literary works, and the Bible;
- understand why the Bible is relevant to the history of imaginative literatures written in English—indeed, why you need to develop basic biblical literacy in order to understand and appreciate substantial segments of most Anglophone literary traditions.

That last goal is especially important as a starting point because it aims to explain why reading this book will be worth your time and effort. It will take me the entire book to explain it thoroughly, but for right now, why should you keep reading?

Here is a preview: to risk stating the obvious, the Bible is the single most influential book in all of Western civilization. Its themes and imagery suffuse Western literary history and have also influenced some non-Western literatures. Literary theory in Europe developed from the study of the Bible, and many landmark texts of modern theory are indebted to it. All this is to say that a basic familiarity with the Bible is nothing less than a prerequisite to understanding the history of literatures written in English.

Such familiarity is also one of the keys to understanding our contemporary world. The Bible is the top bestseller of all time, with more new copies bought each year than of any other book. As global cultural and political issues today are so often shaped by religious worldviews, possessing a basic biblical literacy is a prerequisite to understanding not only literary history but also current events: more than half of the world's religious believers (namely Jews, Christians, and Muslims) trace their faiths to the biblical Abraham. Today, as throughout most of its history, the Bible plays an important role in a wide range of social and political views—from radical to traditional and everything in between.

Yet despite its broad relevance, and despite how many Bibles are sold annually, biblical literacy has been declining for decades. I regularly teach the Bible, and even students who identify as Christian are often shocked to find that they knew very little of it before they started reading it for class.

Should it surprise us that an intensely relevant book is so neglected today, even by those who profess to believe in it? Not really. It is notoriously difficult to read: it is long and repetitive; it can seem boring because its stories seldom tell much about the thoughts and emotions of the characters; its implicit cultural assumptions are often opaque to modern readers; and the complexities of its origins and translation can seem impenetrable. (Unless otherwise stated, the translation used in this book is the New Revised Standard Version, which I chose primarily because it is used in academic study Bibles such as the New Oxford Annotated Bible; for more about different English translations, see Chapter 5 as well as the appendix entitled "A Note on English Bible Translations.") Hence the need for a guide, which is what this book offers. In the process, it also explains how the Bible can help us better understand key aspects of Anglophone literary traditions.

DAVID AND NATHAN: STORIES AS A WAY OF THINKING

The Bible often depicts stories as tools for reflection—as a way of thinking. The best way to explain what I mean by this is to begin by

The word *Bible* derives from the Greek *ta biblia*, which means "the books" or "the scrolls." It is a singular noun in English (and was also singular in an earlier Latin form), but it was originally a plural noun, which is appropriate because the Bible is a collection of books: Protestants include 66; Catholics include 73; and the Eastern Orthodox tradition includes more. Jewish scripture makes up the largest part of the Christian Bible, but Jews count the books differently.

telling a story. You probably know at least one or two good stories that illustrate the saying, "the cover-up is worse than the crime." The Bible offers a juicy example. For starters, the victim in this case is not only innocent but unusually virtuous. In addition, a king once beloved by God and his people sinks to the depths of depravity: in trying to cover up an illicit sexual liaison, he engages in deception, betrayal, and murder. As if that were not enough, the king's downfall is deliciously ironic because he gets tricked into unwittingly condemning his own actions.

The story begins with King David—whom the Bible casts as the greatest king of Israel—walking on the palace rooftop when he spies a beautiful woman, Bathsheba, bathing. He sends for her, but we are not told whether she comes willingly; all we know is that she obeys the king's command and becomes pregnant as a result of their liaison. The king hopes to hide his paternity: perhaps Uriah, her husband, will believe the child is his own. Yet Uriah is off fighting as a member of the king's army, so David orders Uriah home in the hope that he will "lie with" his wife (an ancient Hebrew euphemism for sexual intercourse). Uriah returns to Jerusalem, but his intense loyalty to the Israelite army prompts him to eschew the comforts of his home and wife as long as his fellow warriors continue to fight. Instead, he sleeps on a lowly mat among the king's servants—which is ironic considering that Uriah is not an Israelite but a foreigner, a Hittite, which means that the Israelites look down on him. This highlights David's moral failure: the king should honor those who fight on his behalf, but he turns out to be less loyal and honorable than a foreigner.

To cite a passage from the Bible, use the name of the book as well as the chapter number (these numbers were created in the 13th century CE). You may also use verse numbers (created in the 16th century CE). So "2 Samuel 11:15" refers to the fifteenth verse in the eleventh chapter of the Second Book of Samuel.

David repays Uriah's loyalty with the ultimate betrayal: he sends him back to the front carrying sealed instructions for Joab, the commander of the army, to have Uriah killed. Joab must station Uriah "where the fighting is fiercest"; then he must order the other soldiers to fall back suddenly so that the enemy army slays Uriah (2 Samuel 11). At first, the plan seems to work: Uriah dies in battle, David moves Bathsheba into the palace, and she gives birth to their child. Eventually, however, the truth comes out.

A king's role included adjudicating difficult disputes, and Nathan, the prophet—whose job has less to do with predicting the future than with informing the king about God's will—pretends to tell David about one such dispute. An impoverished Israelite "had nothing" except one lamb, which he loved as if it were his child. A wealthy neighbor stole the lamb—despite the fact that he possessed an entire flock of his own—and had it cooked for a feast. This injustice angers David: "As the LORD lives, the man who has done this deserves to die; he shall restore the lamb fourfold, because he did this thing, and because he had no pity" (2 Samuel 12). To this Nathan replies, "You are the man!"

Nathan's story is more than a politically astute tactic by which to catch the king off his guard. It exemplifies how the Bible uses stories—both fiction and nonfiction—as a way of thinking. Today, researchers in neuroscience, psychology, and narrative theory provide contemporary frameworks for understanding this ancient biblical insight: human beings live within stories inasmuch as we use stories to describe our progressive experience of time passing—event by event, change by change, place by place. In fact, stories do more than merely describe experiences. A story can serve as a conceptual model for making sense of experience or even for taking the measure of it. Such stories include what are sometimes described as "myths," by

> **Narrative Theory** (or narratology) analyzes various strategies and techniques storytellers use. It studies how people interpret stories. More broadly, narrative theory explores how people use stories to make sense of experience. Narrative theory and biblical studies have enjoyed a productive relationship with each other ever since critics such as Jan Fokkelman, Robert Alter, and Meir Sternberg helped elucidate the narrative structure of biblical texts.

which I mean not untrue legends or false stories, as a modern definition of *myth* might imply, but instead stories that articulate the values, beliefs, and worldview of a people. Research shows that when we create or evaluate a story—whether mythical or mundane—we are using a basic and indispensable tool of human cognition. Put simply, human beings use stories to think. Philosophers such as Paul Ricoeur, Alasdair MacIntyre, and Charles Taylor argue that stories constitute a valid and valuable way of thinking. Recent neurological research supports their arguments (to learn more about this research, see David Herman's books listed at the end of this chapter under "Suggestions for Further Reading.")

Consider how the Bible depicts Nathan's fiction as helping David become a less biased judge of his own story. It enables David to imagine himself as an observer rather than a participant. It thereby allows him to imagine the story from the perspective of different participants—including the perspective of a poor man, even though David himself is rich and powerful. Stories can help a reader learn about and identify with different people. This is one of the classic justifications for reading literature, that it can help us empathize with others—walk in someone else's shoes, if you will. This feat of the imagination has its limitations, however, as it can encourage one-sided armchair identification rather than active engagement with others on their own terms. Even so, stories often encourage readers to identify with others in productive ways.

In David's case, the productive turn comes when Nathan pushes David to realize that the story is actually a parable, a brief narrative that seems to be about one thing (its literal meaning) but is about something else (its figurative meaning). By identifying with the poor man, David has identified with Uriah the Hittite, which allows him to see more clearly his own wrongdoing. The word *parable* derives from Greek roots meaning *to cast* one thing *beside* another thing. A parable conveys a moral lesson meant to apply to situations that are analogous or similar to the literal story it tells. Parables exemplify one of the most basic human thought processes, according to Mark Turner. We regularly project one story onto another. Turner argues that our ability to imagine different points of view regarding the same situation also depends on this kind of "parabolic projection."

To turn from a literal to a figurative or analogical meaning, comparing something more concrete with something more abstract, is one of the most fundamental ways in which imaginative literature works. It is also in large measure how the Bible works. At the level of individual words and phrases, the Bible is awash in figurative language. Its literal meanings remain substantially incomplete or even nonsensical if we do not recognize their figurative dimensions: having a "heart of stone" means being stubbornly unresponsive to God (Ezekial 36:26); being an "adulterous generation" means being unfaithful to God (Matthew 12:39); and being offered "living water" means being offered eternal life (Jeremiah 17:13 and John 4:10). Indeed, the Bible regularly uses figurative language to describe God by analogy (by comparison): he is a shepherd, husband, king, lion, and father.

The Bible functions analogically on a larger structural level as well, by suggesting that its component parts—proverbs, poetry, legal codes, expository arguments, and individual stories—derive their fullest meaning from their relationship to the overarching story. Even the Ten Commandments, for example, which might not seem particularly literary at first, begin by explicitly referring to the larger story in which they are set: "I am the LORD your God, who brought you out of the land of Egypt, out of the house of slavery" (Deuteronomy 5; note the figurative use of the word *house*). They implicitly demand to be interpreted as part of that story. Indeed, they refer again to how God freed the Israelites from slavery in order to explain the injunction to rest on the seventh day of each week. The other version of the Ten Commandments—there are two— likewise explains the Sabbath day of rest by referring to another biblical story, namely the account given in Genesis of how God created the world and rested after doing so (Exodus 20).

The Bible often interprets itself this way, so to speak: its component texts frequently refer to each other, suggesting the significance of one part by implicitly or explicitly showing how it repeats another part of the larger whole. So Elijah divides the waters of the Jordan like Moses, who parted the waters of the Red Sea—and like God, who parted the waters in creation (2 Kings 2:8, Exodus 14:21, and Genesis 1:6). Likewise Jesus is cast as a new Adam (1 Corinthians 15:45). Such repetitions frequently interpret the original story figuratively: thus the injunction in Leviticus 25:8–17 for the Israelites to forgive debts and return to their ancestral lands every fiftieth year (the "jubilee" year) gets figured as the return of Israel from defeat and exile to become a great kingdom again in Isaiah 61:1–6. That restoration of the literal kingdom of Israel then gets refigured as a restoration of the spiritual kingdom of God in Luke 4:17–21.

One of the Bible's most striking claims is that its stories are directly relevant to any reader's own life, and indeed that these stories demand a response from the reader. That is to say, the Bible claims an analogical relationship between its stories and the reader's own life story. Thus the Jewish Passover Seder entails retelling the story of how God freed the Israelites from slavery in Egypt, in accordance with the biblical injunction to retell this story for generations to come (Exodus 12–13). The retelling traditionally implies the ongoing power of God to redeem his people in the present as he did in the past.

This kind of analogical relationship is also implicit in the parables Jesus tells in the four Gospels—books in the Bible that tell about Jesus' life and teachings (Gospel means "good news," from the Greek *evangelion*). Consider the parable about malevolent tenants: certain religious authorities among Jesus' listeners immediately relate this parable to their own lives, interpreting the story as implicitly passing judgment on them. The story goes like this: the tenants of a vineyard refuse to give a share of its produce to the owner; instead, they abuse his messengers and kill his son (Mark 12:1–12). To explain the meaning of this parable, Jesus relates it to another biblical text, Psalm 118 (again, the Bible often depicts its stories as repeating and reinforcing each other): "The stone that the builders rejected has become the cornerstone." This is a figurative way of saying that human authorities (the builders) might disobey God and reject Jesus (the stone), but God will eventually right this wrong.

The religious authorities understand that Jesus tells this parable "against them"—that is, they feel judged by it—even though they reject Jesus' authority to judge them. The parable is told within a larger story, the Gospel of Mark, which thus serves as the *frame narrative* for the parable. This larger frame narrative tells the reader that (1) the religious authorities interpret the parable correctly, but (2) they are wrong to reject its authority. That is, the Gospel of Mark strongly insists that Jesus possesses divine authority, but it also (in this episode and many others) repeatedly depicts figures who reject or at least question that authority. Even his ardent supporters question and doubt Jesus. This might prompt readers to think, "What fools!" Yet perceptive readers will realize that they, too, are being challenged to decide whether they accept this story's claims. If not, are they, too, fools? The Gospels thereby present an especially pointed (one might even say pushy) challenge, urging readers to see themselves in these stories much as Nathan urges David, "You are the man!"

Seen in this light, the David-and-Nathan story can serve as a synecdoche (a part taken to represent the whole) that exemplifies a key way in which the Bible uses stories: the Bible repeatedly asks readers to judge themselves much the way Nathan prompted David to judge himself. In short, it claims that its stories apply to the reader's own life. You may accept or reject this claim, but the point is that the Bible depicts stories—fiction as well as nonfiction—as powerful tools for self-reflection precisely because you can interpret them figuratively and analogically. Going further, such ways of interpreting stories have long been considered definitively characteristic of imaginative literature. This, in turn, means that the Bible has an especially close relationship with the literary texts it has influenced.

THE BIBLE AS LITERARY

When I teach a class on this topic, at least one student will insist, "For Christians, the Bible is different from literature: it's holy scripture, a revelation from God. Even if it has literary characteristics, you don't read it the same way you read Shakespeare." Another student will counter, "But if you're not a Christian, then you read them pretty much the same way." A third will add, "Some people read their favorite literary works as if the authors were sort of divinely inspired."

All three make good points. My task is to complicate those points just a bit more. I remind them that even Christians disagree about how to interpret holy scripture. In addition, there is more than one non-Christian way of interpreting the Bible. For starters, Jews interpret Hebrew scripture differently than Christians do even though both consider it holy. Muslims, too, consider parts of the Bible holy but believe the original texts were corrupted. They interpret the Bible in light of the Qur'an, the principal religious text of Islam. There are also a variety of other spiritual and secular ways to interpret the Bible. All such perspectives are potentially relevant when exploring the Bible's influence on imaginative literature. The relevance of any such perspective to a particular literary text depends primarily (but not exclusively) on which perspectives are represented in that text.

Some ways of interpreting the Bible might seem totally incompatible with others, but all of them share at least one significant commonality: they use techniques now associated with literary interpretation. These interpretive techniques are inescapable. After all, the Bible uses them to interpret itself. As discussed above, figurative language pervades the Bible; in addition, many biblical texts implicitly (and sometimes explicitly) interpret earlier biblical texts in figurative or analogical ways. It should therefore come as no surprise that traditional Jewish and Christian ways of interpreting the Bible embrace literary modes of reading. More precisely, they embrace ways of reading that have come to be seen as "literary" but in fact predate the use of that term—indeed, in Christian tradition the term was "spiritual." Figurative readings of the Bible that would now be considered "literary" were called "spiritual" readings. In the words of an early Christian leader, Paul, "the letter kills, but the Spirit gives life" (2 Corinthians 3).

A traditional Jewish way of interpreting Hebrew scripture, called *midrash*, likewise seems quite literary by modern standards. Midrashim typically expound on difficult scriptural passages where there seems to be insufficient explanation or a gap in the story. By paying careful attention to small details and drawing not only on other scriptural texts but also other midrashim, a rabbi (a religious leader and teacher) helps resolve or clarify a textual complexity.

Scholars such as Geoffrey Hartman place this ancient Jewish way of interpreting scripture in conversation with contemporary literary criticism, arguing that the two traditions of textual interpretation bear illuminating similarities to each other.

The Jewish philosopher Philo of Alexandria (c. 15 BCE – CE 50) commended *allegory* as a method of interpreting Hebrew scripture. The letters of Paul use this method—more precisely described as *typology*. By the third century CE, typology and allegory had become staples of Christian interpretation. Philo drew on Greek and Roman thinkers who interpreted their myths as allegorical representations of abstract ideas. Paul interprets the scriptural story of Abraham's two sons in a similarly figurative way: Ishmael represents the law given to Moses on Mount Sinai (including the Ten Commandments), whereas Isaac represents faith in Christ (Galatians 4:21–31). Paul attributes figurative, non-literal meanings to literal elements of the earlier stories such as characters and events.

By the twelfth century CE, Christians had created a complex method of interpreting the Bible that involved four levels of

ALLEGORY VERSUS TYPOLOGY

In allegorical readings, each major element of a story figuratively represents a second meaning; together, these figurative meanings create a second "level" of significance to the story. So in Nathan's story, the poor man represents Uriah the Hittite and the rich man represents David. Some allegories represent abstract ideas rather than historical events, but in either case, the literal level of the story is often fictitious and is generally less important than the figurative level. Typological readings, by contrast, do not lessen the significance of a text's literal meaning but only add a figurative level to it. So Paul's reading of the Abraham story does not undermine the literal meaning of that story but only adds a new, figurative level of meaning to it in light of the Jesus story. (In practice, sometimes the distinction between allegory and typology gets fuzzy.)

meaning: (1) the literal; (2) the typological, by which any biblical passage could be related to the story of Jesus; (3) the tropological, which focused on discerning a moral to be applied to the reader's or listener's daily life; and (4) the anagogical, which related to the anticipated end of history and return of Jesus. Thus, for example, the long history of the city of Jerusalem could be interpreted as referring to (1) the historical city; (2) the history of the followers of Jesus and the development of Christianity; (3) the personal story of any Christian; (4) the heavenly city of God to be established at the end of history. Eventually, this figurative method of biblical interpretation contributed to the development of a highly esteemed type of English literature: allegory. An author purposefully suggests figurative meanings to each major element of a story so that, together, they create a second "level" of significance. Famous examples include William Langland's *Piers Plowman* (late fourteenth century), Edmund Spenser's *The Faerie Queene* (1596), John Bunyan's *The Pilgrim's Progress* (1678), and George Orwell's *Animal Farm* (1945).

All this is meant to illustrate my earlier claim that the Bible's literary characteristics are not anathema to religious interpretations but rather constitute an integral aspect of its long reception history. Indeed, the Bible has influenced Western literary traditions so extensively that many aspects of those traditions have biblical origins—including major strains of literary criticism, as scholars such as Stephen Prickett point out. This book aims to help readers learn about this complex history.

Today, **hermeneutics** refers to the methods or "rules" by which we interpret any kind of text. When it was first used in the 18th century, however, it applied only to the methods used to interpret the Bible. **Exegesis** refers not to the general rules of interpretation but to a specific interpretation of a specific text; it, too, originally referred to interpretations of biblical texts, even though it now can refer to an interpretation of any kind of text.

FORM AND CONTENT

"What is it about?" When discussing imaginative literature, the answer to that question usually focuses on *content*: plot, characters, and themes. Content answers a "what" question whereas *form* answers a "how" question: "How is the story told?" The answer will focus on *formal qualities* such as the type of narrator (e.g., first-person or third-person), the plot structure (e.g., chronological or non-chronological), or the writing style. A basic tenet of literary criticism holds that form and content shape each other.

To that end, it will help to distinguish among three different domains in which the Bible's literary influences may be traced:

1   allusion
2   resonance
3   broad cultural trends

ALLUSION

The first mode, allusion, is the easiest to detect for readers who are familiar with the Bible. An allusion is a reference to another text or historical figure or event. It can be direct or indirect, easy or difficult to catch (depending on a given reader's knowledge and how explicitly an author makes such a reference). An allusion to the Bible might be a quotation of a biblical phrase or passage; the name of a biblical figure or place; a biblical symbol, image, or plot; or a stylistic quality such as diction or syntax that is characteristic of the Bible— that sounds like the Bible, so to speak (Chapter 5 focuses on this and other formal aspects of the Bible, especially the influential style of the Authorized or King James Version, abbreviated KJV).

In Shakespeare's *Hamlet*, for example, the title character at one point refers to the biblical figure of Cain by name, reminding the audience that Cain committed "the first murder" (5.1.77). Abel was killed by his less-virtuous brother, Cain, which serves as a fitting parallel to Shakespeare's story about the murder of Hamlet's father by his father's less-virtuous brother, Claudius (Genesis 4). The murderer himself alludes to the story of Cain and Abel but in slightly less obvious terms: Claudius complains that he has brought "the primal eldest curse" upon himself by "a brother's murder" (3.3.40). In Shakespeare's day, most of his audience probably knew that God curses Cain for the murder. Claudius pleads, "Is there not rain enough in the sweet heavens / To wash [this bloody hand] white as snow?" (3.3.45–6). This one is more subtle: Hannibal Hamlin argues that Shakespeare alludes here to a line from Psalm 51, "wash me, and I shall be whiter than snow" (Isaiah 1:18 also uses this image).

Today, some might think of Pilate washing his hands to proclaim that he is innocent of Jesus' "blood" (Matthew 27:24). After all, bloody hands are not mentioned in Psalm 51. Most audiences today would have difficulty catching the Psalms allusion, which was probably easier for Shakespeare's original listeners: people were legally required to attend church services, and Psalms were read at every service. The first audiences were likely to remember that most of the Psalms are traditionally attributed to King David; a few might have recalled that Psalm 51 is set immediately after Nathan the prophet has confronted David for committing adultery and having Uriah killed. David, like Claudius, wishes God would forgive him for murdering the innocent man whose wife he subsequently married.

J. K. Rowling offers an instructive contemporary example of a biblical allusion in *Harry Potter and the Deathly Hallows* (2007). Harry finds a Dumbledore family tombstone bearing this inscription: "Where your treasure is, there will your heart be also" (325). A Bible-savvy reader will recognize this direct quotation from Matthew 6:21. Most readers likely miss this allusion, although Rowling leaves a clue for those with ears trained to hear the archaic syntax of the KJV. Some modern translations try to maintain the old-fashioned beauty of the phrase but update the syntax slightly: "there your heart will be also." The signature sound of the KJV can be illustrated by contrast with a resolutely contemporary translation: "Your heart will always be where your treasure is."

Recognizing biblical allusions can help you understand a literary text more fully. Not only can each allusion clarify the author's "intentions"—a tricky concept on which I elaborate shortly—but also the overall patterns of biblical allusions can help reveal an author's allusive practices. Does the author favor direct allusions, indirect ones, or a mix of the two? What difference does that tendency make—why might the author have chosen it? To what aspect of the Bible does the author typically allude? Must a reader know the larger biblical context of the allusion in order to understand its role in the literary text, or is the allusion's relationship to the new context less specific, functioning more by vague suggestion? Finally, do the allusions function harmoniously with traditional interpretations of the Bible, or do they subvert such interpretations?

When we spot explicit biblical allusions (as in the above examples), we typically infer that the author purposefully created those allusions. Could Rowling have used the line from Matthew in her novel without realizing it was from the Bible? Possibly, but not likely. Even so, how Rowling intended the reader to interpret the allusion might depend in part on the extent of her own knowledge of the Bible, which can be quite difficult to determine. The best evidence usually comes from the literary work itself: if an author alludes frequently to the Bible, as Shakespeare does, then we have stronger evidence that he knew it well and purposefully chose each allusion. As I tell my students, establishing a pattern of evidence makes for the strongest case; it is best to avoid making strong interpretive claims based on only one example.

RESONANCE

The second mode of biblical influence, resonance, overlaps with allusion but describes instances sufficiently vague that it is difficult to determine the author's intentions or even whether the author was aware of the possible allusion. "Resonance" is an acoustic metaphor: the term evokes the way in which a sound produced by one object elicits sympathetic vibrations in a second object such that it produces a complementary sound. The two together create tones that are more prolonged and harmonically complex than either one could produce alone. The second object may not be *designed* to resonate with the first, but it must be designed in such a way that it *can* resonate with the first—not just any object will resonate. Indeed, the particular form of the second object will determine the kinds of resonance it can produce.

So it might be that a reader hears a biblical resonance where an author did not, but such cases can still be worth considering because of the Bible's extraordinarily pervasive cultural influence: its sounds are everywhere. An author might have unwittingly or even subconsciously incorporated biblical imagery, themes, or language into a literary work. Perhaps the reception history of that work was influenced by its readers' perception of biblical resonance even if the author did not intentionally or even subconsciously create such resonance. Such possibilities would be improbable if we suspected, for example, that a twenty-first-century novel vaguely resonated with a less influential text such as Thomas Gray's *Elegy Written in a Country Churchyard* (1751). When it comes to the Bible, however, a vague resonance may well be an important factor in the design or reception of a given literary work.

Take *Hamlet*. Given the allusions discussed above—to the stories of Cain and Abel, David and Uriah, and Pilate and Jesus—might not the play tacitly imply larger parallels with all three of these stories? The larger stories are not precisely the same, but they do resonate with each other. For example, Shakespeare's play depicts the murder of a virtuous person as calling out for judgment by supernatural means: a ghost reveals the murder to Hamlet and demands justice. Similarly, Abel's blood cries out to God (Genesis 4:10); God sends Nathan to condemn David (2 Samuel 12:1); supernatural portents after Jesus' death prompt witnesses to acknowledge his innocence (Matthew 27:51–4); and supernatural inspiration prompts Peter to call for the repentance of those who were complicit in Jesus' death (Acts 2). On another note, Hamlet feigns madness to protect himself from a murderous king's wrath, which resonates with an earlier episode in the life of David when he, too, feigns madness (1 Samuel 21:10–15). And Hamlet creates a story (in the form of a brief play) to trick King Claudius into revealing his guilt, not unlike Nathan's story that tricks David into condemning himself. The two are not the same: Hamlet's story is a reenactment in which Claudius quickly recognizes himself, whereas Nathan's story is an allegory whose figurative meaning remains hidden to David until Nathan reveals it. Yet they resonate with each other, testifying to the power of artful stories.

In the case of J. K. Rowling's novels, many readers identify Harry Potter as a Christ figure based on a series of approximate parallels between the two. A vicious adult tries to kill the infant Harry for fear of a prophetic claim that the boy will grow into a rival, which recalls King Herod's efforts to kill Jesus because of the prophetic claim that Jesus will be a king (Matthew 2). Harry is later revealed to be a "chosen one" who possesses special powers. And in *Harry Potter and the Deathly Hallows*, Harry must willingly sacrifice himself by allowing his enemy, Voldemort, to kill him. Harry then gets resurrected (it turns out that he never truly died) in order to save the world by defeating Voldemort. In this, he is depicted as conquering death by learning not to fear it, which, according to his friend, Hermione, means learning to trust in the hope of "living after death" (328). Hermione offers this explanation in response to a quotation on the headstone at the graves of Harry's parents: "The last enemy that shall be destroyed is death." The quotation comes from 1 Corinthians 15:26, a direct allusion, whereas the parallels with the larger story of Jesus remain approximate. Unlike Jesus, Harry does not actually die and is not God. It seems very likely that Rowling purposefully created resonant parallels with the Gospel stories, but it also seems likely that she purposefully avoided making her story an explicitly and definitively Christian one.

A DIGRESSION INTO LITERARY THEORY

At this point, I need to address a thorny problem underlying much of the above discussion—namely, that of inferring an author's intentions. Before explaining the third way in which the Bible influences literature, we need to explore brief versions of some theoretical debates that have preoccupied many literary critics over the past seventy-five years. The pay-off will be not only to clarify the distinction between allusion and resonance but also to introduce concepts that will help clarify the third mode of influence, broad cultural trends.

In the 1940s, W. K. Wimsatt and Monroe C. Beardsley introduced "the intentional fallacy." They argued that we should not concern ourselves with the author's intentions when trying to understand a work of literature. Instead, the text itself, if it has been well constructed, should make those intentions sufficiently clear without recourse to extra-textual information about the author's life or opinions. This argument exemplified "the New Criticism," a movement that championed internal coherence as a hallmark of great literature. If a text achieves internal coherence—even if that coherence arises out of ironic tensions—then the text by itself can articulate its implicit values and meaning.

By the late 1960s, however, critics such as Roland Barthes and Michel Foucault cast doubt on whether any literary text could achieve the kind of internal coherence lauded by the New Critics. These later scholars agreed that the author's intentions are irrelevant when interpreting a work of literature—but not because those intentions should be clear from the text alone. It was rather because, in their view, it is impossible for even the most skillful author to create a text that conveys one clear and coherent meaning. They contended that language is inherently incoherent, despite that language might seem to be a systematic structure designed to communicate meaning. This type of thinking is often called *poststructuralist* because it uses concepts developed by earlier analyses of the structure of language-systems, but it employs those concepts to undermine the earlier claim that linguistic structures can convey clear, definite meaning. According to the type of interpretive practice made famous by Jacques Derrida, we can *deconstruct* the illusion of coherent meaning in literary and other texts. To do so, we reveal the text's subtle self-contradictions and inconsistencies.

Scholars have criticized poststructuralism and deconstruction on a variety of grounds. While the complexities of such debates lie beyond the scope of this book, two key insights developed from these schools of thought hold considerable significance for the topic at hand.

First is *intertexuality*, the idea that any given text creates meaning by explicitly and implicitly citing, alluding to, and resonating with other texts, as well as by using linguistic and literary conventions which, by definition, it shares with many other texts. Other texts thus form the background or context necessary for readers to make sense of a given text. Some definitions of intertextuality are more radical than others, but for our purposes, the general notion helps describe the way in which so many biblical texts allude to or resonate with other biblical texts. Taken as a whole, the Bible creates more complex meanings through this kind of intertextuality among (and sometimes intratextuality within) its component parts. Intertextuality also helps describe the Bible's influence on imaginative literature: if the Bible has been a prominent part of a particular cultural context, then it is more likely to have an intertextual relationship (whether explicitly or implicitly) with other texts created and read in that context.

The second insight derives from deconstruction, which holds that any given text constructs meaning in ways that overtly or covertly reinforce the socioeconomic power hierarchies of its cultural context. This is a more troubling way to conceptualize the "power" of stories: individual texts—including literary texts no less than religious, medical, or legal ones—tend to reinforce socioeconomic hierarchies by echoing binary oppositions that distinguish insiders from outsiders, or "centers" from "margins." Such binaries include male versus female, citizen versus foreigner, rich versus poor, self versus other, healthy versus sick, and natural versus unnatural. Deconstruction seeks to expose the unexamined assumptions typically reinforced by such binaries: it argues that what might seem to be a "natural" and simple distinction in fact performs the artificial and complex cultural task of privileging some and excluding others.

A deconstructive lens can be highly revealing when it comes to the Bible. This is a text that frequently endorses binaries but also loves to flip them upside down and question them. In terms of its reception history, the Bible has served as a rallying cry for the outcast and oppressed but also as a "clobber text" used to support nationalism, racism, anti-Semitism, sexism, homophobia, slavery, the abuse of animals, and the mistreatment of people with disabilities. These complexities are reflected in the Bible's literary legacy, as Chapter 4 explains.

Taken together, these two insights—regarding intertextuality and the socioeconomic exclusions reinforced by common binary oppositions—help clarify an important limitation to the idea of authorial intention: authors create literary texts not in a vacuum but in a cultural context that informs their creations. Authors therefore do not have absolute control over what they create. Their intentions are only part of the story; another important part concerns the ways in which any literary work is inevitably and often unintentionally informed by its context. To search for these unintended aspects of a literary work is called *symptomatic reading*, which Porter Abbott distinguishes from *intentional reading* (trying to discern the author's intentions) or *adaptive reading* (creating a new text inspired by but not focused on the original text).

If we focus too much on authorial intention, we can overlook cultural influences. We also risk oversimplifying the creative process, which can be intuitive in ways that elude conscious planning and control. Nevertheless, attempting to infer the intentions of a speaker or writer is something people do every day, and we regularly get it mostly right. Our inferences may not be perfectly or exhaustively accurate (especially in the case of complex statements or translations between different linguistic and cultural contexts), but evidence shows that they are regularly accurate enough. Every day, people manage to understand each other well enough to work and play together.

Acknowledging the tendency for readers to infer the intentions of an author, narrative theorists distinguish between the flesh-and-blood author and the *implied author*, a term that denotes the sense of authorial intention readers typically infer from a text. David Herman suggests that we instead think of texts as blueprints from which readers construct meaning. The building metaphor helps remind us that while intentional design shapes texts, readers must perform extensive work to create meaning—say, a story—in their minds. Such a story thus ultimately derives from a collaborative process that involves both author and reader.

BROAD CULTURAL TRENDS

These concepts help explain why interpretations of the Bible have historically changed as their cultural contexts changed, which brings us to the third domain in which the Bible influences imaginative literature: broad cultural trends. Identifying an allusion or resonance entails focusing on an individual literary text, but this third mode seeks to identify how the Bible has influenced many texts in similar ways within the same broad cultural context.

Take the claim I made earlier, that the medieval Christian practice of interpreting the Bible typologically and allegorically helped give rise to the prominence of allegory as an esteemed genre or literary form. This kind of claim is necessarily somewhat speculative because it depends on making large-scale generalizations. It is much easier to find strong evidence to support the claim that a specific text alludes to another specific text. Nonetheless, identifying broad cultural trends can be quite useful, provided that our conclusions remain more or less provisional depending on the strength of the available evidence.

We may claim with a high degree of certainty, for instance, that Shakespeare likely expected his audiences to be quite familiar with the stories and sayings of the Bible. He also likely expected a bigger potential "bang" from biblical allusions than twenty-first-century authors can expect. Religion was far more intimately connected with politics in sixteenth- and seventeenth-century England, and the stakes could literally be a matter of life and death. We gain a better understanding of the biblical allusions and resonance in *Hamlet* if we understand this aspect of the play's original cultural context.

Consider another example. In the eighteenth century, the novel was on the rise as a popular literary form in England, but it was not yet a highly respected form—not until the Bible helped confer respectability on it in the nineteenth century. Stephen Prickett contends that the novel came to be seen as a legitimate art form in the nineteenth century in part because people began to interpret the Bible much as they interpreted novels. Such "novelistic" interpretations may predate the nineteenth century, but many novels in that era did adopt a tone sufficiently religious as to allow readers to associate novels with biblical narratives. In terms of their reputation as an art form, novels gained by the association. In addition, it is possible that the Bible served as an important model for long, complex Victorian novels whose many different characters and seemingly disparate storylines came together, in the end, to reveal their thematically harmonious interconnections as if by providential design. After all, many Victorians interpreted the Bible as revealing a providential unity in its many disparate parts.

By the later nineteenth century, a growing number of literary critics and authors championed the aesthetic qualities of the Bible—its purely formal, artistic beauty—while treating its literal meanings as merely the invented legends of "primitive" cultures. While the Bible's formal qualities had been influencing authors for centuries, the nineteenth and twentieth centuries witnessed a significant number of literary works that evince primarily formal rather than thematic biblical influences. Chapter 5 focuses on these formal influences, arguing that they became increasingly "ghostly" in the twentieth century for a number of reasons—not least being readers' declining familiarity with the specific formal features of the KJV.

In the later twentieth century, Northrop Frye hailed the Bible as "the great code" of Western literature and art, the defining myth of Western culture. He also described the language of the Bible as "visionary." Frye's terms—*great code, myth, visionary*—arguably reflect a cultural trend of the nineteenth and twentieth centuries in which some hoped that beautiful literature might take the place of traditional religious belief. Frye's terms impart a vague sense of the possibility of transcendence and redemption. A more recent literary critic, Amy Hungerford, similarly argues that a vague, anti-doctrinal sense of religion informs important strains of twentieth-century literature.

I prefer to describe the language of the Bible as *figurative* rather than visionary because the former term seems compatible with a wider range of secular and religious perspectives. Likewise, the idea of the Bible as the source text of Western art can imply an overly simplistic and unidirectional model of intertextual influence. That idea does not adequately acknowledge the extent to which the Bible's literary legacy was shaped by its larger reception history, which includes not only artistic but also political and social history. As Chapter 4 explains, for example, the Bible's immense influence on Anglophone literatures owes not only to its own intrinsic merits but also to the immense power once wielded by the British Empire.

An additional problem with the idea of the Bible as the great source text is that the Bible is not always the original or most important intertext. For starters, the Bible itself incorporates earlier influences. Additionally, readers interpret the Bible in ways that often reflect other influences: sometimes what seems to have originated with the Bible might actually have originated with, say, Milton's seventeenth-century depiction of Satan in *Paradise Lost*, or John Darby's nineteenth-century notion of "the rapture." Finally, certain stories and themes in the Bible share so much in common with other cultural traditions and texts that in some cases the Bible is more accurately understood as one voice among many in a larger conversation, so to speak—not the source of that conversation.

In Rowling's Harry Potter novels, the Bible functions like a prophetic yet ghostly voice from the past—not the ghost of a murdered king calling for vengeance as in *Hamlet* but a more intertextual ghost, rarely making a definitive appearance, and even then only as a still mysterious yet illuminating tombstone inscription. In this regard, the Harry Potter novels exemplify much contemporary literature, showing the Bible's influence especially in their thematic resonances with that ancient text. This book aims to illuminate the Bible's legacy in contemporary literature as much as in earlier periods of literary history, which is why the first four chapters explore major biblical themes—each of which can be described in terms recognizable to Harry Potter fans: the sense of mystery and wonder, the importance of friendship, the struggle against injustice, and unexpected kinds of heroism.

WHAT TO EXPECT FROM THE REST OF THIS BOOK

After this introduction, the next chapter—Chapter 1—summarizes the overall story told in the Bible. It also explains how the Bible can be understood as a collection of texts that were originally created separately but were later compiled into a single book. In addition, each of the first four chapters explores a set of related texts from the Bible, selecting those texts according to shared themes: otherworldly stories that cannot be told fully or clearly (Chapter 1); stories about intimate relationships (Chapter 2); stories about what happens when those relationships get betrayed and broken (Chapter 3); and stories about how such relationships get restored and recreated (Chapter 4).

These first four chapters focus on major themes not only because these themes have been especially influential in contemporary literature but also in the hope that these four thematic categories will help you mentally organize the vast number of texts that make up the Bible. By seeing how different biblical texts can be grouped together in four categories, even readers with little prior knowledge of the Bible can develop an accessible interpretive framework for exploring the meaning of a wide variety of biblical texts. Grouping these texts together can also help illuminate the Bible's insistent intertextuality. In case you get lost in the details, the conclusion of each chapter offers a bullet-point summary of that chapter's main points.

Each of the first four chapters addresses a number of literary works as examples of how the themes explored in that chapter have influenced different types of imaginative literature. Literary works often invoke multiple biblical themes, so some works discussed in one chapter may also be relevant to another chapter. This introductory chapter focuses on two of the most widely known authors—Shakespeare and Rowling—in an effort to make the subject more relatable for the widest array of readers. By contrast, subsequent chapters include a more diverse range of texts. In order to include such a range while also providing a comprehensive overview of the Bible itself, I have limited the discussions of individual literary works to brief glimpses. I hope to entice you to read at least some of these literary works. The annotated suggestions for further reading at the end of each chapter direct you to more extensive analyses of many of the literary works mentioned in that chapter as well as other relevant primary and secondary readings.

Throughout the book, I try to maintain a productive tension between interpreting the Bible as a unified whole and interpreting it as a collage of different texts and viewpoints—which often means maintaining a tension between traditional religious interpretations and alternative readings from within as well as outside those traditions. Indeed, this complex tension between unity and diversity constitutes one of the larger stories told by *The Bible and Literature: The Basics*. Understanding both sides of this tension is useful not only because each side helps us understand the other but also because the tension itself helps explain why the Bible has inspired such a diverse array of authors.

While this introduction and the first four chapters are designed to be read in order, the fifth chapter may be read out of sequence. Some readers will prefer to jump right into the biblical stories told in Chapter 1, but others may choose to take a detour to Chapter 5 to learn about the history of English Bible translations and their formal influences on both the English language in general and imaginative literature specifically.

The conclusion first looks backward, tying together the preceding chapters. It then looks forward by answering questions about the ongoing literary influence of the Bible in the present and near future. Some might assume that the Bible's literary influence is declining due to the decline of religion more generally in our "secular" age. A range of contemporary thinkers help challenge that assumption. The Bible continues to be intensely relevant to contemporary literature—although not necessarily in the ways some might expect.

SUMMARY

- This book is for those who want to learn more about the Bible and its influence on imaginative literatures in English.
- The David-and-Nathan story helps illustrate a key way in which the Bible uses stories as a tool for self-reflection— as a way of thinking.
- People interpret the Bible differently depending on whether or not they consider it to be holy scripture. Regardless of religious beliefs, however, everyone must use interpretive techniques now considered literary in order to make sense of the Bible.
- The two preceding points, coupled with the Bible's pervasive currency in English-speaking cultures, help explain why the Bible has influenced imaginative literatures in English so profoundly. Its influence on such literatures can be divided into three overlapping modes: (1) allusions, (2) resonance, and (3) broad cultural trends.
- William Shakespeare's *Hamlet* and J. K. Rowling's Harry Potter novels help illustrate these three modes.
- An overview of the rest of the book helps prepare the reader to get the most out of *The Bible and Literature: The Basics*.

QUESTIONS FOR DISCUSSION

1   What do you think of when you hear someone mention the Bible? What values do you associate with the Bible? What values do you think others associate with the Bible?

2   Some claim that the Bible today is one of the most published and least read books. What do you think are some of the most common misperceptions about the Bible?

3   Some people are more easily captivated and moved by stories than others (psychologists describe such people as "highly transportable"). Have you ever been deeply moved by a story? Was it fiction or nonfiction? Has a story about someone else ever

helped you think through a problem in your own life? Are there limits to using stories in that type of way?

4   What differences or similarities do you see between imaginative literature and the Bible? How much does your answer to this compare-contrast question depend on which works of imaginative literature and which specific biblical texts you consider? What differences might others see between imaginative literature and the Bible?

5   The Bible has influenced works of literature that reflect a wide range of religious and secular (non-religious) worldviews. Why might an atheist or agnostic author choose to include allusions to the Bible in a novel, poem, or play? Why might a Christian, Jewish, or other religious author choose to include biblical allusions?

SUGGESTIONS FOR FURTHER READING

To continue your exploration of the topics discussed in this and other chapters, consider reading one or more of the literary and biblical texts mentioned. Doing so will give you a fuller understanding of the necessarily brief descriptions provided in this book. It will also help you raise your own questions and draw your own conclusions.

For relevant Bible readings in addition to those mentioned in this chapter, try other parables such as the ones found in 2 Samuel 14:1–21, 1 Kings 20:38–43, or the many recounted in Matthew, Mark, and Luke.

For relevant nonfiction works, consider the following:

Alter, Robert and Frank Kermode, eds. *The Literary Guide to the Bible*. Cambridge, MA: Harvard University Press, 1987. This collection of essays offers a book-by-book tour of the literary qualities of the Bible.

Carruthers, Joe, Mark Knight, and Andrew Tate, eds. *Literature and The Bible: A Reader*. New York: Routledge, 2013. A collection of excerpts from scholarly works published over the past few decades, this reader aims to provide an overview of the development of the contemporary study of the relationship between the Bible and literature. Of the scholars addressed in this chapter, it contains excerpts from works by Hans-Georg Gadamer, Geoffrey Hartman, Robert Alter, Stephen Prickett, Jacques Derrida, and Northrop Frye.

Ciaccio, Peter. "Harry Potter and Christian Theology." *Critical Perspective on Harry Potter*. Ed. Elizabeth E. Heilman. Abingdon, UK: Routledge, 2009 (2nd ed.). 33–46. Ciaccio shows how the Harry Potter novels resonate with various concepts and traditions in Christian theology.

Hamlin, Hannibal. *The Bible in Shakespeare*. Oxford: Oxford University Press, 2013. A thorough exploration of biblical allusions in Shakespeare's plays, this study also illuminates the rich biblical culture of Elizabethan and Jacobean England.

Herman, David, James Phelan, Peter J. Rabinowitz, Brian Richardson, and Robyn Warhol. *Narrative Theory: Core Concepts and Critical Debates*. Columbus, OH: The Ohio State University Press, 2012. This multi-authored book introduces readers to the complex and growing field of narrative theory. For a detailed account of how various fields of study contribute to understanding narrative as a basic function of the human mind, see David Herman, *Storytelling and the Sciences of Mind*. Cambridge, MA: MIT Press, 2013; for another such account, see Mark Taylor's *The Literary Mind*. Oxford: Oxford University Press, 1996.

Jeffrey, David Lyle, ed. *A Dictionary of Biblical Tradition in English Literature*. Grand Rapids, MI: William B. Eerdmans, 1992. This is an encyclopedic reference guide to biblical themes, symbols, phrases, and names in terms of their influence on English literature. It also contains useful bibliographies.

Lieb, Michael, Emma Mason, and Jonathan Roberts, eds. *The Oxford Handbook of the Reception History of the Bible*. Oxford: Oxford University Press, 2011. This collection of essays offers a guide to many different aspects of the Bible's reception history.

Norton, David. *A History of the English Bible as Literature*. Cambridge: Cambridge University Press, 2000. This revised and condensed version of Norton's larger two-volume work surveys the five-hundred-year history of English Bible translations, focusing on changing estimations of the literary qualities of these translations.

1

WRESTLING WITH GOD: THE BIBLE AS AN UNTELLABLE TALE

Who wrote the Bible? What were their aims?

This chapter explores three common answers to these questions. In doing so, it provides a multi-layered framework for understanding individual biblical texts within their larger contexts. It also explains how these three answers have influenced literary history.

While it is quite possible to subscribe to more than one of the following answers at the same time, they are worth distinguishing from one another because they each describe a different aspect of the Bible and its reception history. Yet as I detail in this chapter, each one offers a variation on a theme shared by all three: in different ways, they all imply that the Bible attempts to tell a story that cannot be told.

1   **The history of a people.** The Bible chronicles the history of the rise and fall of Israel, followed by a spiritual restoration of the Israelite kingdom through Jesus. A traditional view holds that the texts of the Bible were written by those who participated in various stages of this history—by contemporaries or near-contemporaries of the events described.

2   **A story about God.** The Bible chronicles God's interactions with human beings such that God may be seen as the main

"character," if you will. There are many different theories about what "divine inspiration" might mean, but in general, Christians and Jews have traditionally believed that the various authors of the Bible were inspired by God such that their writings reveal aspects of God's nature as well as God's plan for humankind.

3   **A collection of fragments.** Since the 1700s, scholars have amassed substantial evidence suggesting that the Bible was written by many different people with different aims, and that many of these writers were born long after the events they describe. Various editors later refashioned these writings such that we no longer have direct access to the earlier compositions in their original forms. According to this view, the Bible as it now stands is a mosaic composed of textual fragments that reflect different theologies, cultures, and worldviews. Most of these fragments remain partially "buried" under rewritings and editing as well as later traditions of interpretation that render it difficult to uncover the contexts and meanings of the original source material.

Many people subscribe to more than one of these three views at the same time. For example, Christians and Jews have traditionally viewed the Bible as both the history of a people and a story about God. Even so, it can be useful to distinguish between the two because each one describes an aspect of the Bible that has, at times, received greater emphasis. To take another example, many people in recent centuries have viewed the Bible as a collection of fragments that nevertheless tells a divinely inspired story about God. They read the stories less as history than legend, but they read these legends as conveying mythic truths about God. For still others, the fragmented view undermines any belief in divine revelation as well as any strong sense of historical accuracy.

When I teach the Bible, students are often most interested in the question of its historical accuracy. The answer to that question depends on which biblical text we are discussing, but the answer also depends on what we mean by "historical accuracy." Modern readers often assume a forensic sense of "history" by which truth is determined in the most scientific way possible, but we must remember that this reflects a modern understanding of history. We can certainly ask such modern questions of ancient texts, but we should keep in mind that, in doing so, we are imposing anachronistic distinctions that can obscure earlier understandings of these texts.

For instance, the Bible's reception history attests to a high tolerance in the ancient world for different versions of history. The Bible offers two different accounts of creation (Genesis 1:1–2:3 and 2:4–3:24, although some read these as one account); two slightly different versions of the Ten Commandments (Exodus 20 and Deuteronomy 5); two different histories of the rise and fall of the Israelite kingdom (1 Samuel – 2 Kings and 1 & 2 Chronicles); and four different versions of the life of Jesus (the four Gospels: Matthew, Mark, Luke, and John). Early Christians recognized that the four Gospels contradict one another on various minor points—Tatian's *Diatessaron* (c. CE 160–75) was one of the first attempts to synthesize them into one unified account—but all four Gospels have generally been embraced by Christian traditions despite how they differ from one another. Indeed, their differences have sometimes been seen as contributing to a greater truth.

While all this illustrates an older, less forensic sense of history, it does not mean that the question of historical accuracy is entirely anachronistic. While the ancient world showed greater tolerance for multiple versions of history, history was not considered fiction—merely legendary. On the contrary, every stage of the Bible's reception history attests to the importance of a mix of both figurative and literal interpretations, as exemplified in the traditional four levels of interpretation described in the introduction to this book. Literal interpretations typically assume that the historical narratives in the Bible are accurate. Only in modern times have large numbers of English-speaking readers interpreted the Bible as merely legendary.

Miracles constitute another complicating factor for modern readers when trying to answer the historical accuracy question. When students ask me whether a given biblical story is true, they are sometimes simply asking whether non-biblical sources (such as other ancient texts or archaeological evidence) corroborate the biblical account. Often, however, they really want to know whether I believe the many biblical depictions of miracles.

For the purposes of this book, what matters is the wide variety of beliefs about the Bible that have influenced literary history. Which of these various beliefs matter most at any given moment depends on which literary text we are considering at that moment—namely, the beliefs the text explicitly or implicitly represents as well as which beliefs helped inform the context of that text's composition or reception history. Happily, therefore, my task is not to tell you which parts of the Bible should be interpreted literally and which parts figuratively, let alone whether miracles exist (for more about miracles, see Chapter 4). Instead, my aim is descriptive rather than prescriptive—to survey various common answers to such questions and explain how they have shaped the literary reception history of the Bible.

This is no cheap dodge or evasion of controversial questions. On the contrary, one of the central arguments of this book is that the Bible's extraordinary influence—its literary power—derives in part from the wide variety of ways it has been interpreted. *Not* to explore and appreciate the tensions and commonalities among different ways of understanding the Bible, I contend, is to misunderstand its literary reception history. Indeed, the same principle applies to its larger (not just literary) reception history. The Bible regularly challenges its readers to respond to it (as discussed in the last chapter), so ignoring the most common ways in which people have *actually* responded to it means ignoring how the Bible "works," so to speak.

The three views of the Bible outlined above help illuminate various answers to the complex question of the Bible's historical accuracy. The rest of this chapter elaborates on these three views, emphasizing each one's literary legacy. In doing so, this chapter reveals a common thread shared by all three: each view suggests that the Bible attempts to tell an untellable tale—a story that by necessity remains both unclear and incomplete.

THE HISTORY OF A PEOPLE

Conceptualizing the Bible as one overarching storyline can distort this complex collection of texts by imputing greater harmony to it than might actually exist, in effect oversimplifying it. Yet such a "grand narrative" of the Bible can also help us organize and therefore more easily remember the component texts even if we later complicate or even undermine the sense of harmony. In addition, the unifying "grand narrative" merits attention because it has played a prominent role in the reception history of the Bible.

One traditional way to describe the overarching story told in the Bible focuses on the rise, fall, and spiritual restoration of Israel. That history begins with Abraham. What comes before Abraham—the first ten and a half chapters of Genesis—can be seen as the prologue or backstory, which includes the creation of the world, the sin of Adam and Eve in the Garden of Eden, Cain's murder of Abel, Noah and the flood, and the Tower of Babel. These stories set the stage for God choosing to create "a great nation" from Abraham's descendants (Genesis 12:2), a nation that will be enslaved in Egypt for four hundred years (Genesis 15:13) but will then be given the fertile "land of Canaan for a perpetual holding" (Genesis 17:8). God makes a covenant or binding agreement with Abraham according to which, in return for Abraham's loyalty, God will create this special nation—later called Israel—from his descendants. As a sign of the covenant, Abraham and his wife, Sarah, receive new names (they had been Abram and Sarai), and Abraham and his male descendants must be circumcised.

The first six books of the Bible recount this covenant and its fulfillment. Abraham's descendants become Israel, God's chosen people, who eventually settle in Canaan, the promised land. Abraham and his son and grandson, Isaac and Jacob, are commonly referred to as the Patriarchs, the forefathers of Israel. God gives Jacob this new name, Israel, after Jacob wrestles with God (or an angelic representative of God) to secure a blessing: Israel means "one who strives with God" (Genesis 32). Jacob's twelve sons become the forefathers of the twelve tribes of the nation, Israel (the names of the tribes are listed slightly differently in different places, e.g., Numbers 1 versus Revelation 7).

The story of Joseph tells how a famine prompts Jacob's sons to travel to Egypt (Genesis 37–50). They settle there and prosper; many generations later, however, they become enslaved to the Egyptians. Moses leads the Israelites out of bondage in Egypt into the desert, at which point God renews the original covenant and adds a far more elaborate set of requirements that include the Ten Commandments. Eventually, Joshua leads Israel across the River Jordan into the promised land, thus fulfilling God's original covenant with Abraham.

The next stage of this history describes the rise of the monarchy. Its greatest king is David, but even he is flawed (as discussed in the

CHRONOLOGY OF MAJOR STAGES OF BIBLICAL HISTORY

(The dates with question marks are highly disputed.)

The Patriarchs: Abraham, Isaac, and Jacob	c. 1800 BCE?
Exodus from Egypt (Moses)	c. 1250 BCE?
Israel emerges in Canaan	c. 1200–1025 BCE
United Monarchy: Saul, David, and Solomon	c. 1025–928 BCE
Divided Monarchy (Israel and Judah)	c. 928 BCE
Israel falls	c. 722 BCE
Judah (Jerusalem) falls	c. 586 BCE
Exile in Babylon ends	c. 538 BCE
Second Temple period begins	c. 520 BCE
Jesus of Nazareth	c. 4 BCE–CE 30
Second Temple destroyed	c. CE 70

previous chapter): at the height of his powers, David sows the seeds of his kingdom's decline. Thus it comes as no surprise that David's son, Solomon, builds a glorious temple to God but later turns away to worship other gods. Like his father, Solomon's weakness derives from his intemperate sexual desires. Even in his weakness, however, David's heart remains true to God whereas Solomon's does not (1 Kings 11:4).

With a few exceptions, Solomon's heirs lead the Israelites even further astray. The twelve tribes become divided: ten tribes form a separate Kingdom of Israel in the north, while the tribes of Judah and Benjamin form the Kingdom of Judah in the south. As the kings and their subjects in both territories become increasingly corrupt, God allows them to be vanquished by neighboring foes. The Kingdom of Israel falls first, conquered by the Assyrians. Eventually Jerusalem and its magnificent temple get destroyed by the Babylonians, and the leaders of the Kingdom of Judah are forced into exile in Babylon.

The books of Ezra and Nehemiah tell how the sixth-century BCE Persian King Cyrus releases the Judeans or Jews (so-called because they hail from the former Kingdom of Judah) from their Babylonian captivity and allows them to return to Jerusalem and rebuild their temple. Thus begins what historians call the "Second Temple Period." The Judeans continue to be controlled by foreign powers except for brief periods during the second and first centuries BCE, after which they are ruled by the Romans. The Judeans, the remnant of Israel, hope that a great king from the line of David will arise to restore Israel to its former glory. They call this hoped-for king the Messiah, meaning the "anointed one," because one becomes king not by being crowned but by being anointed with oil. The Greek translation of *Messiah* is *Christos*—in English, *Christ*.

The final section of the Bible is called the New Testament or Covenant (the original Greek term may be translated either way) because it develops from and renews the covenants God made with Abraham and Moses (Luke 22:20). The New Testament focuses on telling the story of the Messiah, the long-hoped-for king, Jesus of Nazareth. The Gospel of Matthew, the first book of the New Testament, drives this home by tracing Jesus' lineage from David and summarizing that lineage with prophetic symbolism: it counts fourteen generations from Abraham to King David (the high point of the Kingdom of Israel), then another fourteen from David to the Babylonian captivity (the low point), and then a final fourteen generations to Jesus the Christ (Matthew 1:17). Yet in an ironic twist, the return of the king does not restore the Davidic throne. Rather than lead the Judeans to victory over the Romans as expected, the Christ ends up crucified—killed by Roman authorities. After his miraculous resurrection, however, his followers come to see Jesus as heralding the "kingdom of God," a spiritual kingdom that will be fully realized only at the end of history.

Put simply, the Bible tells a story that remains incomplete. By definition, its conclusion must be deferred until the end of history. The final book of the Bible, the Revelation to John, offers a symbolic vision of the coming kingdom of God (Revelation 21). The gates and foundations of this kingdom bear the names of the twelve tribes of Israel and the twelve disciples of Jesus, which implies that the promise to Abraham will be finally and completely fulfilled in the future when Christ returns. The book of Revelation focuses primarily on the frightening cataclysms that will precede the advent of this kingdom; as for the kingdom itself, Revelation offers not much more than the assurance that there will be no more pain or death and that this new kingdom will be like a restored Garden of Eden (Revelation 21–2).

In keeping with this vague depiction in Revelation, the four Gospels suggest that the kingdom of God is difficult if not impossible to comprehend. Jesus uses figurative language (most often parables) to describe the kingdom, and his disciples frequently misunderstand these teachings. Indeed, his explanations sometimes seem purposefully designed to confuse, as when he avers, "It is easier for a camel to go through the eye of a needle than for someone who is rich to enter the kingdom of God." His disciples interpret this as impossible: "Then who can be saved?" Jesus reassures them, "For mortals it is impossible, but for God all things are possible" (Matthew 19:23–6).

The Old Testament similarly suggests that its story about God remains partially untellable, that God cannot be fully described or explained in human terms: "To whom then will you liken God, or what likeness compare with him?" (Isaiah 40:18). Like the New Testament, it uses what we would consider literary devices such as figurative language to convey the limitations of what it can tell. After all, what better way to describe something indescribable than by comparing it with something that *can* be described? So the promised land is "a land flowing with milk and honey" (Exodus 3:8), much as the "river of the water of life" will flow through the city of God when his kingdom comes (Revelation 22:1–2). These descriptions point beyond their literal meanings to an abundance beyond ordinary imagining.

The Israelites repeatedly fail to understand that no human king can lead them successfully to the abundance God plans for them, much as the disciples repeatedly fail to understand that Jesus is not merely a human Messiah. Both stories make sure that the attentive reader does not fail to understand these things, thus creating a sense of dramatic irony found frequently in biblical stories. Gideon specifically warns the Israelites that their only king should be God, but they disregard him (Judges 8:22–3). When the Israelites later persuade the prophet Samuel to anoint their first human king despite Samuel's warnings, they fail to recognize that their own argument implicitly undermines itself. They insist that they need a king because Samuel's sons (who have become judges over Israel) are not good leaders like Samuel is, but a human king's son would inherit his

> **Dramatic irony** occurs when the reader or audience knows more than the characters know. The readers thus understand the characters' words or actions differently than the characters themselves do. (For a fuller definition of **irony**, see the beginning of Chapter 4).

throne and would be no less likely to disappoint (1 Samuel 8:1–9). Eli, the good priest who led Israel before Samuel, also had sons who were "scoundrels" and corrupt leaders (1 Samuel 2:12). Why do the Israelites expect a king's sons to be different?

The narrative thus casts the Israelites as remarkably dense, which is how the Gospels depict the disciples. Yet the point seems not that the Israelites or disciples are less intelligent than other people but rather that God's kingdom is remarkably difficult for anyone to understand. Consider how Psalm 23 figures God as a shepherd who cares deeply for his sheep. David, the greatest king of Israel, was originally a shepherd; as a king, he describes his human subjects as sheep (2 Samuel 24:17). Jesus, too, refers to himself as a shepherd (e.g., in John 10). Like the dramatic irony in the biblical narratives about the Israelites and disciples, this metaphor potentially casts the sheep-like people in an unflattering light: sheep are not known for their intelligence. In the context of the Bible, however, the king-as-shepherd metaphor reinforces biblical depictions of the vast difference between humans and God as well as God's caring for people despite their imperfections.

Even Moses, who understands God more clearly than any other prophet (Numbers 12:6–8), falters in his belief and disobeys God (Numbers 20:12). As a result, he cannot enter the promised land. The significance of this punishment is arguably clearer in Jewish traditions, which hold the first five books of the Bible to be the holiest texts in Hebrew scripture. These five books together are called the Pentateuch by Christians and the Torah by Jews (Pentateuch means "five scrolls"; Torah means "instruction" or "teaching" and can also refer to rabbinic commentary on those five books). The Torah ends not with the fulfillment of the Abrahamic covenant by the triumphal entry of Israel into the promised land but rather with God showing

Hebrew scripture is often referred to as **Tanakh**, an acronym for Torah, Nevi'im (the Prophets), and Ketuvim (the Writings): T + N + K.

Moses that land from a distance and reminding him that he is not allowed to enter it (Deuteronomy 34:4). In short, Torah depicts the nation promised to Abraham as something hoped for and even glimpsed from afar but not yet fully attained.

The rest of Hebrew scripture similarly casts the chosen nation in this partially ineffable light as an ideal not yet fully obtained. The sixth book, Joshua, describes Israel's violent and ultimately victorious conquest of the other peoples living in Canaan, the promised land. Yet the seventh book, Judges, suggests a less victorious and more unfaithful Israel: Abraham's descendants turn away from God and against each other (as they do repeatedly in the Torah, as well). Judges seems designed in part to justify the need for a human king. It chronicles the increasingly disturbing sins of the people when "there was no king in Israel" such that "all the people did what was right in their own eyes" (Judges 21:25). When kings finally arise in the books of Samuel and Kings, however, they will not keep the Israelites from turning away from God.

If we read the Bible as a unified history of God's people, then this overarching narrative takes on a familiar plot structure. It begins by depicting a state of equilibrium: God creates a peaceful and orderly world in which human beings have "dominion" over all the other creatures. Humans are made in God's "likeness" and rule the world as if they were vice-regents for God (Genesis 1:26). An inciting incident then creates conflict, thus initiating what literary critics commonly term the rising action: Adam and Eve disobey God's command not to eat fruit from the "tree of the knowledge of good and evil," so God expels them from the garden of Eden (Genesis 2–3). Yet God softens their punishment. Despite his warning to Adam—"in the day that you eat of it you shall die"—he does not kill them that day but lets them live for nearly a thousand years. Similarly, eating the fruit causes them to feel ashamed about their nakedness, but God makes clothes for them. Thus begins a long and complex series of conflicts, bad choices, and partial resolutions—always followed by renewed conflicts—that build from the inciting incident, "the fall" of Adam and Eve. Despite their failures, God keeps inviting humans back into a harmonious relationship with him. This is the basic plot, a story repeated throughout the Bible like variations on a musical theme in a complex symphony.

For Christians, the climax of this overarching narrative arrives with the crucifixion and resurrection of Jesus. Christians believe that God thereby restores a harmonious relationship with humans once and for all. The falling action describes the creation of the first Christian communities. It also looks forward to the rest of human history as an extension of this falling action, anticipating the dénouement—the final outcome of the story—when Christ returns to finish establishing the kingdom of God on earth. This overarching plot structure emphasizes that the ending remains tantalizingly half-glimpsed but nonetheless suspended, held in abeyance as a promised but still not completely fulfilled hope.

UTOPIA / DYSTOPIA

The literary legacy of this overarching biblical narrative has especially influenced the genre inaugurated by Sir Thomas More's fictional creation of an impossibly perfect society, *Utopia* (1516, originally published in Latin). While some have read More's work as a revision of Plato's *The Republic*—the famous fourth-century BCE account of a perfect government—others have interpreted More's *Utopia* as implying a biblical insistence that such an ideal cannot be achieved by merely human efforts. More coined the word *utopia*, and he acknowledged that this neologism plays ironically with its Greek roots. While it sounds like *eu-topia*, which would mean "good place," its "u" evokes *ou topos*, meaning "no place." It represents a human ideal that cannot be fully realized.

It seems therefore appropriate that the genre inspired by More's *Utopia* eventually created *dystopian* fiction, as well. Seeming utopias often turn out to be dystopias—not the best but the worst societies, typically dominated by inhumane governments that oppress their subjects in the name of order and stability. The Bible is not the origin of utopian and dystopian fiction, nor has it directly influenced the entire genre. Yet such stories resonate richly with the Bible when they allude to it. Famous examples that directly allude to the Bible include Aldous Huxley's *Brave New World* (1932), William Golding's

The Lord of the Flies (1954), and Margaret Atwood's *The Handmaid's Tale* (1986). (Some dystopian fiction also resonates with apocalyptic writings from the Bible; such writings are addressed in Chapter 3.)

Just because these novels allude to the Bible does not necessarily mean they promote a traditional religious worldview. Some of them, such as *The Handmaid's Tale*, implicitly criticize what they cast as dangerous propensities in such worldviews. Indeed, dystopian fiction may owe less to the Bible than to most readers' appetite for conflict—perfection can be boring! In any case, the Bible often serves as a provocative intertext in dystopian fiction because it resonates especially with the tension between the ideal of a perfect society and the reality of human imperfection.

The Bible's kingdom narrative has also influenced less extreme literary representations of the aspirations and failures of societies. For example, William Faulkner's *Absalom, Absalom!* (1936) casts the southern United States as Israel. After the American Civil War, many southerners regarded the pre-Civil War or Antebellum South nostalgically as an Edenic "golden age." According to the novel's depiction, however, that "golden age"—like David's reign (the title refers to his son, Absalom)—doomed itself to future destruction because of its moral failings. The novel highlights racism, slavery, and economic class prejudices as signs that the Antebellum South was far from perfect. Casting a nineteenth-century plantation patriarch as a modern David, the novel chronicles his rise and fall.

Joseph Conrad's *Heart of Darkness* (1899) invokes the Bible in its depiction of British imperialism in Africa. Yet Conrad's opinion of that history seems far more ambiguous than Faulkner's opinion of U.S. history. By contrast, Chinua Achebe's *Things Fall Apart* (1959) offers a pointed critique of imperialism in biblical terms. The Igbo people at first welcome British colonists, but the colonists soon turn out to be as destructive as the plague of locusts that "cover the face of the land" in Exodus 10. Achebe offers a complex and nuanced portrayal of Christian missionaries and their role in British colonization, which illuminates his portrayal of the aspirations and failures of the British Empire more broadly. It was neither the first nor the last empire to cast itself in glorified terms as if it were God's chosen people. One could argue that no empire has proved itself less prone to human failings than the biblical Kingdom of Israel.

A STORY ABOUT GOD

Thus far, we have seen how the Bible can be read as a history of Israel, but there is more to it than that. Another common way of reading the Bible emphasizes God as the main "character," so to speak. Rather than seeing the opening chapters of Genesis as a prologue, this view finds the focal point of the Bible in its opening words: "In the beginning when God created the heavens and the earth ..." Such an emphasis does not ignore the history of Israel but rather illuminates a different aspect of the Bible's reception history—an aspect shaped even more insistently by the tension between what can and cannot be told.

The Bible often represents God in paradoxical ways that suggest he is unrepresentable: God is a fire that does not burn, a voice composed of silence, and a thunderous question with no answer. These images have come to be associated with the notion that God is *transcendent*, beyond everyday experience. Yet the Bible sometimes uses more familiar imagery, describing God as a father, husband, or king. Such images have become associated with the notion that God is *immanent*, existing in intimate relationships with everyday experience. Some Jewish and Christian traditions have emphasized God's immanence; others, his transcendence. For the most part, however, the two have generally been viewed as interrelated aspects of God rather than mutually exclusive characterizations.

Even so, it can be productive to explore each aspect separately at first. This chapter focuses on biblical depictions of God's transcendence while the next focuses on depictions of his immanence. The richness of the interplay between the two types of imagery becomes

Transcendent describes something beyond ordinary human experience and understanding. When describing God, it typically also expresses the idea that God exists beyond or outside of material existence. **Immanent** refers to something familiar to ordinary human experience, and it often expresses the idea that God is not wholly separate from but also exists within the material world.

> Jacob was left alone; and a man wrestled with him until day-break. When the man saw that he did not prevail against Jacob, he struck him on the hip socket; and Jacob's hip was put out of joint as he wrestled with him. Then he said, "Let me go, for the day is breaking." But Jacob said, "I will not let you go, unless you bless me." So he said to him, "What is your name?" And he said, "Jacob." Then the man said, "You shall no longer be called Jacob, but Israel, for you have striven with God and with humans, and have prevailed." (Genesis 32)

clearer if we first appreciate the richness within each type. Once the two are well established in Chapters 1 and 2, their complex interplay unfolds in Chapters 3 and 4.

To get started, consider the story of Jacob wrestling with a man-like angel—or with God—which I mentioned above in my brief overview of the history of Israel. One night, Jacob wrestles with "a man" who is actually a divine being (an angel, according to Hosea 12:4). This being then renames Jacob. Scholars debate the etymology of the new name, *Israel*, but according to the story it refers to his successful struggle with God (Genesis 32). (The suffix *-el* in names such as Israel, Michael, Gabriel, and Daniel derives from *El*, an ancient word for God.)

The wrestling story illustrates the Bible's paradoxical portrayal of God. On the one hand, God is like a person with whom one can wrestle and even hope to prevail—much as Jacob's grandfather, Abraham, prevailed when he argued with God over the fate of Sodom (Genesis 18). Jacob's descendant, Moses, similarly prevails when he convinces God to provide him a helper to lead the Israelites (Exodus 4), and again when he dissuades God from destroying the Israelites completely (Exodus 32), and yet again when he persuades God to show his glory (Exodus 33). *Israel* is indeed a fitting name for this family.

On other hand, however, God is far too powerful to be defeated. So even though Jacob "prevails" by gaining a blessing, Jacob leaves this fight limping. In addition, his new name indicates who really

There the angel of the LORD appeared to him in a flame of fire out of a bush; he looked, and the bush was blazing, yet it was not consumed. Then Moses said, "I must turn aside and look at this great sight, and see why the bush is not burned up." When the LORD saw that he had turned aside to see, God called to him out of the bush, "Moses, Moses!" And he said, "Here I am." Then he said, "Come no closer! Remove the sandals from your feet, for the place on which you are standing is holy ground." ... Moses said to God, "If I come to the Israelites and say to them, 'The God of your ancestors has sent me to you,' and they ask me, 'What is his name?' what shall I say to them?" God said to Moses, "I AM WHO I AM." (Exodus 3)

has the power here: naming or renaming someone in the ancient world meant having power over that person. Thus Adam names the other creatures in Genesis 2 because he has been given dominion over them. Conversely, when Jacob asks the name of his combatant after the wrestling bout ends, God or the angel refuses to tell.

The untold name here resonates with the first *theophany* (an appearance of God) to Moses. Moses turns aside to investigate an extraordinary sight: a bush is on fire but appears unburned, unblackened by the flames. God speaks to Moses there, and the name God calls himself is as paradoxical as a fire that does not burn: "I AM WHO I AM" (Exodus 3). The original Hebrew may have suggested the past, present, and future tenses of the verb *to be* at the same time, in effect conveying a sense of being as large as existence itself. The name potentially teases us out of thought not only because it is not a proper noun but also because it stymies our attempts to make sense of it. Like going barefoot in the desert (see inset), it defies common-sense expectations.

One finds a similarly arresting sense of strangeness in a more common biblical name for God, which gets transliterated into English using four consonants—YHWH—but which traditionally has been considered too holy to be spoken aloud by pious Jews. Scholars refer to YHWH as the Tetragrammaton, the four letters. It appears

Now Mount Sinai was wrapped in smoke, because the LORD had descended upon it in fire; the smoke went up like the smoke of a kiln, while the whole mountain shook violently. As the blast of the trumpet grew louder and louder, Moses would speak and God would answer him in thunder. (Exodus 19)

in most English Bible translations as "the LORD" (in all capital letters) in keeping with an ancient tradition in which Jews substitute "Adonai" (meaning "my Lord") for the not-to-be-spoken name. (Using "G-d" instead of God is a more contemporary way of signaling this form of respect for the mystery of God.) "Jehovah" may derive from combining the vowels of *Adonai* with a Latin transliteration of the Tetragrammaton: JHVH. Scholars debate whether YHWH etymologically derives from a form of the Hebrew verb meaning "to be, become, make happen." In any event, the tradition of not speaking it aloud resonates with the burning-bush episode: God's name is paradoxically present and absent, there and not there.

The Bible depicts other theophanies using similarly extraordinary and even paradoxical imagery. When God delivers the Ten Commandments on Mount Sinai, for example, even the height of the mountain, which symbolizes God's transcendent power (like the "ladder" or stairway Jacob witnesses in Genesis 28), points beyond itself insofar as the mountain trembles "violently" under God's grandeur (Exodus 19). The presence of God remains shrouded in fire and smoke much as God led the Israelites out of slavery in Egypt in the form of a pillar of cloud by day and fire by night (Exodus 13). His voice, as he speaks to Moses, is described as "thunder."

The miraculous change wrought in Moses frightens his fellow Israelites: "the skin of his face shone because he had been talking with God" (Exodus 34). He begins to wear a veil because even just this reflected afterglow of God's glory proves too much for his compatriots to bear.

The New Testament echoes this theophany in that Jesus delivers the core tenets of his new covenant from a mountain in Matthew

5 (this "sermon on the mount" occurs not on a mountain but on a level plain in Luke 6, a difference we return to shortly). The Gospels further echo the story of Moses when Jesus becomes transfigured by the glory of God on a mountain and God speaks from a cloud: the face of Jesus "shone like the sun, and his clothes became dazzling white" (Matthew 17). When Moses speaks with God on Mount Sinai, the Israelites are confounded and fearful. In the New Testament, Jesus' disciples play that role—not surprisingly, as the twelve disciples represent the twelve tribes of Israel (even though only three of the twelve accompany Jesus to his transfiguration). Indeed, when God or one of his angels appears to a human, the ostensibly reassuring "do not be afraid" (as in Luke 1:30) also reminds careful readers that the Bible consistently depicts humans as feeling overwhelmed by God's presence.

While Jesus has traditionally been seen as exemplifying God's immanence, his partial accessibility through ordinary human experiences, the story of Jesus also emphasizes God's transcendence. His transcendent aspect can be seen not only in his transfiguration and difficult teachings but especially in his miraculous resurrection. The Gospels insist that Jesus' disciples cannot comprehend or believe in his resurrection until some time afterwards when it slowly begins to dawn on them that Jesus' kingship differs radically from that of any human king.

Indeed, in case we too easily or simply associate God with human kings, fire, light, mountainous height, or thunderous sound, the Bible undermines all of this imagery by repeatedly insisting that God "dwells in thick darkness" (1 Kings 8). Even if we associate God with "the heavens," the holiness of the temple, or the ark of the covenant (which contains the Ten Commandments written by "the finger of God" on two stone tablets, according to Deuteronomy 9:10), we also find other biblical stories about God that question such assumptions: "Will God indeed dwell on the earth? Even heaven and the highest heaven cannot contain you!" (1 Kings 8).

When God appears to the prophet Elijah, who is on the run from the wicked King Ahab and his manipulative wife, Jezebel, the imagery similarly emphasizes God's transcendence. As the King James translation famously puts it, God speaks in "a still small voice," using old definitions whereby *still* means silent and *small* means thin or sheer. Is a voice of thin silence really a voice? Or in the New

> [God] said, "Go out and stand on the mountain before the Lord, for the Lord is about to pass by." Now there was a great wind, so strong that it was splitting mountains and breaking rocks in pieces before the Lord, but the Lord was not in the wind; and after the wind an earthquake, but the Lord was not in the earthquake; and after the earthquake a fire, but the Lord was not in the fire; and after the fire a sound of sheer silence. (1 Kings 19)

Revised Standard Version (see inset), what is the sound of silence? Likewise, is an unsayable name really a name? Is a fire still a fire if it does not burn? Generations of religious believers have seen the Bible as inviting readers to wrestle with these questions as a way of wrestling with God. Like Nathan confronting David, the imagery confronts readers by at first seeming to be about one thing but then pointing beyond itself to something else—a partially indescribable something that purports to make a claim on readers like Nathan's parable makes a claim on David.

The Book of Job offers an illuminating example of this biblical theme. Job questions why God allows terrible things to happen to good people. Finally, God appears and, like a wrestler, turns Job's question back on itself: How can you hope to understand a

> Then the Lord answered Job out of the whirlwind:
> "Who is this that darkens counsel by words without knowledge? Gird up your loins like a man, I will question you, and you shall declare to me.
> "Where were you when I laid the foundation of the earth? Tell me, if you have understanding. Who determined its measurements—surely you know! Or who stretched the line upon it? On what were its bases sunk, or who laid its cornerstone when the morning stars sang together and all the heavenly beings shouted for joy?" (Job 38)

transcendent God? How could I give you an answer you would understand? While his thunderous answer sounds at first like a rebuke, God actually approves of this attempt to wrestle with him (metaphorically) in the form of Job's honest insistence that he does not understand. By contrast, God strongly rebukes the false complacencies of Job's friends who think they understand God perfectly well (Job 42). Like Moses in the desert and Elijah on the run, Job encounters God through his struggles.

Taken together, these theophanies represent one of the most fascinating aspects of the Bible. The main character remains shrouded in mystery:

> My thoughts are not your thoughts, nor are your ways my ways, says the LORD. For as the heavens are higher than the earth, so are my ways higher than your ways and my thoughts than your thoughts.
>
> (Isaiah 55; see also chapters 40 and 44)

In the New Testament, Paul explains,

> We know only in part, and we prophesy only in part; but when the complete comes, the partial will come to an end. When I was a child, I spoke like a child, I thought like a child, I reasoned like a child; when I became an adult, I put an end to childish ways. For now we see in a mirror, dimly, but then we will see face to face. Now I know only in part; then I will know fully.
>
> (1 Corinthians 13)

The Ten Commandments prohibit creating an "idol," an image worshiped as if it were a direct representation of God. It makes sense, therefore, that the Bible represents God indirectly through metaphors, symbols, parables, and analogies while repeatedly reminding the reader that none of these figurative representations fully expresses the nature of God.

The Bible is inherently literary in this sense. It uses word-pictures and stories to point beyond themselves. This also helps explain why figurative (non-literal) interpretations of the Bible have traditionally been called spiritual readings: they aim to illuminate spiritual truths that, by definition, can be expressed only figuratively.

PROFOUND MYSTERIES OR MYSTIFYING ILLUSIONS?

Shakespeare draws on this biblical tradition in his wonderfully fantastical comedy, *A Midsummer Night's Dream* (c. 1596), in which various characters find themselves transported to a magical fairy realm. In a speech by one of these characters, a comic ham named Bottom, Shakespeare intentionally misquotes the Bible as Bottom tries to articulate his unbelievable fairyland adventures:

> I have had a dream, past the wit of man to say what dream it was ... The eye of man hath not heard, the ear of man hath not seen, man's hand is not able to taste, his tongue to conceive, nor his heart to report, what my dream was.

> (4.1.215–24)

In literary criticism, *synesthesia* means describing one kind of sensory experience in terms of a different kind (e.g., "hot pink" uses the sense of touch to describe a visual perception). Yet Bottom is not using synesthesia but is simply getting it wrong, comically mixing different types of sensation. As noted in the introduction, Shakespeare's original audiences would have been more likely to catch the biblical allusion in this joke: "What no eye has seen, nor ear heard, nor the human heart conceived, [is] what God has prepared for those who love him" (1 Corinthians 2).

While *A Midsummer Night's Dream* might seem to use the Bible for merely comic effect, it may well be up to something more complicated. The play offers a whimsical meditation on romantic love, especially on whether "true love" really exists. Perhaps true love is an illusion, like a dream or even a kind of madness. Alternatively, there might be something more to romantic love even if that "something" cannot be pinned down or proved. Bottom misquotes the Bible, but his allusion may not be inappropriate. Romantic love might be like the biblical portrayal of God—too strange to comprehend fully and too important to ignore.

To trace the impact on modern literature of the Bible's depictions of divine transcendence, the key starting point lies with the English Romantic poets. Scholars debate whether the term "Romantic" accurately describes their work. They were poets not so much of romantic love but of powerful feelings in general. These late eighteenth- and early nineteenth-century poets felt that ordinary "common-sense" views of their world lacked a vital dimension. In trying to articulate that dimension, they often turned to the Bible.

Consider William Wordsworth's *Tintern Abbey* (1798), which mourns the wild, exuberant joy Wordsworth remembers feeling when he was a child. Now trapped in a disenchanted world of adult worries and responsibilities, he finds a grown-up form of consolation in what he describes as the "still, sad music of humanity." Here, the "still, small voice" of God, which reassured Elijah when he was in despair, becomes the paradoxically silent music of a woeful human race, which reassures Wordsworth. We might interpret this woeful but spiritual music as invoking the traditional Christian belief that a person in need or in despair is God, in some sense (Matthew 25). Perhaps it suggests instead a non-Christian sense of spirituality in human beings. In either case, the "still, sad music of humanity" seems to lead to profound joy and peace as Wordsworth describes an intuition or feeling of a spiritual "presence" that presides over and animates all existence:

> . . . I have felt
> A presence that disturbs me with the joy
> Of elevated thoughts; a sense sublime
> Of something far more deeply interfused,
> Whose dwelling is the light of setting suns,
> And the round ocean and the living air,
> And the blue sky, and in the mind of man;
> A motion and a spirit, that impels
> All thinking things, all objects of all thought,
> And rolls through all things.
>
> (*Tintern Abbey*, 94–103)

The passage resonates with 1 Kings 8 (cited above) in which God's "dwelling" (some form of this word appears seven times in that chapter of the KJV) is everywhere and nowhere. God's transcendence is suggested by the paradoxical description of this "spirit" as omnipresent yet somehow ineffable, "a sense sublime / Of something" elusive but profound.

Even Percy Shelley, a self-avowed atheist, found inspiration in the Bible's depictions of transcendence. In his *Mont Blanc* (1817), the tallest Alpine mountain represents something like *Tintern Abbey*'s spiritual presence—"the secret strength of things inhabits thee"—but Shelley locates this hidden power not in the mountain but in the mind of the poet who contemplates the mountain. This distinction draws on Platonic thought as well as eighteenth-century notions of the sublime, which held that the power of nature (as evident in a violent storm at sea or an awe-inspiring mountain) could evoke a startling feeling of pleasure as well as terror, as if the human mind were more powerful than nature on some level and could therefore enjoy the terrifying spectacle. In keeping with this notion of the sublime, Shelley poses a rhetorical question at the end of the poem: What would Mont Blanc amount to—indeed, what would even the "earth, and stars, and sea" amount to—"If to the human mind's imaginings / Silence and solitude were vacancy?" The implied answer is *nothing*.

Yet to the human mind, the poem suggests, even the sound of silence is not nothing. In the Bible, the prophet Elijah stands on a mountain and witnesses a powerful and even terrifying scene of violent winds, earthquakes, and fire, but all that serves merely to get his attention. The epiphany comes when he realizes that the real power lies in the silence. Somehow in that silence he hears the voice of God. In *Mont Blanc*, the poet witnesses the terrifying grandeur of a mountain, but it, too, turns out to be merely a device to get his attention. The poet's epiphany comes as he recognizes his own imagination in his experience of the mountain, the same imagination that can fill the vacancy of silence. The poet in effect becomes a prophet—not of God but of the imagination.

Wordsworth, Shelley, and other Romantic poets helped give rise to the widespread modern assumption that the most serious forms of imaginative literature aim to articulate truths so profound that they can be represented only figuratively. The Romantics' use of biblical imagery accompanied this development so that the modern artist, no longer simply a skilled artisan or intellectual observer, became a kind of prophet. This is not the only modern conception of what it means to be an artist, but it remains a prevalent one.

Modern literary criticism also took the imprint of Romanticism in some respects, encouraging literary critics to cast themselves in the role of prophets. Many late twentieth-century critics justified their embrace of arcane theoretical language on the grounds that their insights were so profound as to defy conventional language. They insisted that conventional language and common-sense understandings of reality mask obscure truths.

Some have accused such literary critics of engaging in linguistic sleight-of-hand to create the illusion of profound mysteries that turn out to be merely cheap mystifications. This charge has also been leveled against Romantic poets and their artistic descendants, some of the most famous of whom might be called prophets of popular music. Bono, the lead singer of U2, insists that "mystery and mischief" are the two essential ingredients of rock 'n' roll. A sense of mystery can be manufactured merely for the sake of trying to hook an audience, not only in pop music but also in literature. While crime novels and the like generally depict solvable mysteries, many readers expect "serious" literature to depict unsolvable mysteries that occasion profound insights. The difference between works of literature that achieve such insights versus those that achieve only an empty sense of mystification lies to some extent in the eye of the beholder.

A COLLECTION OF FRAGMENTS

So, too, with the Bible's depictions of God as a transcendent mystery: some find they amount to little more than mystification. Where some see a divine puzzle, others see a disconnected assortment of textual fragments that do not cohere into a unified whole unless by artificially imposed force. This is a secular way of describing the Bible not as the story of a people or a story about God but as an ancient mosaic.

Consider the story of Jacob wrestling with the angel from this perspective. Earlier in the chapter, I interpreted that story in terms of how it resonates with other biblical stories. This kind of interpretation assumes that the various biblical texts are related to each other and therefore can help illuminate each other—as if they were composed by a single author who crafted the story intentionally and successfully so that his intentions could be discovered by careful reading. Religious interpreters have traditionally assumed that the various authors of the Bible shared enough of a common inspiration that the texts they created fit together as one generally unified whole. Thus, for example, repetitions among different biblical texts of themes, images, key words, or plot structures have been interpreted as suggesting purposeful and meaningful patterns even if the individual authors might not have intentionally created such patterns.

What if we look not for unity but for diversity among biblical texts? What if the texts reflect the fact that the Bible was composed by a large number of different authors from different historical periods and cultural contexts? What if the texts produced by the original authors were later edited together in ways meant to suggest purposeful and harmonious intertextual relationships but that, if analyzed closely, also reveal substantial discord among the worldviews that shaped these different texts? During the past few centuries, scholars have increasingly embraced this approach. According to this modern view, the Bible is a collection of disparate fragments.

For example, the story about Jacob wrestling with the angel includes discordant elements that potentially undermine the assumption that this episode was penned by the author of the Bible's other Jacob stories. Why, for starters, does the text narrate the crossing of the river Jabbok twice? At first, Jacob seems to cross the river with his family: "The same night he got up and took his two wives, his two maids, and his eleven children, and crossed the ford of the Jabbok" (Genesis 32:22). In the next lines, however, the family crosses without Jacob: "He took them and sent them across the stream, and likewise everything that he had. Jacob was left alone" (Genesis 32:23–4). Is this a poetic repetition not meant to be taken literally, or might the second crossing reveal the beginning of a story from a different source that was later edited into the larger story about Jacob?

Furthermore, why must the angel or divine being depart before daybreak? No other story in the Bible limits angels in this way. Yet such limitations do appear in legends from the ancient Near East about human encounters with night demons. According to many scholars, the most plausible explanation is that this story originated as just such a legend, perhaps blending a night-demon tale with a river-god tale. If so, then the legend was later incorporated into Israelite scripture, a new context that changed the demon or demigod into an angelic representative of YHWH.

Jacob's encounter with the angel is what scholars refer to as a *pericope*, a brief section of the Bible that can be read as a self-contained story or unit of text. One can find many such examples throughout the Bible that may have come from an earlier source. The "Sermon on the Mount," for instance, appears only in Matthew and Luke but is somewhat different in each. Most scholars believe that the Gospel writers drew this episode from an earlier source, which they then adapted in slightly different ways to fit their respective narratives. In Luke, the speech takes place on a level plain, but in Matthew, it takes place on a mountain (Luke 6, Matthew 5). In Luke, the Beatitudes (blessings) emphasize literal poverty—"Blessed are you who are poor"—but in Matthew, the message is spiritualized and set in the third person: "Blessed are the poor in spirit." Luke similarly has "Blessed are you who are hungry now, for you will be filled," while Matthew has "Blessed are those who hunger and thirst for righteousness, for they will be filled."

Close examination of such similarities and differences among the four gospels has led scholars to describe Matthew, Mark, and Luke as the Synoptic Gospels because they can easily be "seen together" (the literal meaning of *synopsis*) in the sense that they share so much in common. In contrast, the Gospel of John is quite different. Most likely, the writers of Matthew and Luke both drew on Mark. They also probably both drew on another source (the hypothetical "Q" from the German *Quelle*, meaning "source"), which contained the Beatitudes as well as other sayings of Jesus.

Scholars have similarly hypothesized a variety of sources for the Torah or Pentateuch, the first five books of the Bible: Genesis, Exodus, Leviticus, Numbers, and Deuteronomy. Traditionally referred to as the Five Books of Moses, they were long thought to have been authored by Moses himself. Since the seventeenth century, however, scholars have questioned this tradition. By the late nineteenth century, Julius Wellhausen's "documentary hypothesis" became the dominant scholarly view: it views the Pentateuch as an edited compilation of various narratives that were originally independent of one another.

While the specifics of the hypothesis are not directly relevant to the topic at hand, one aspect of it usefully complicates a topic already broached in this chapter: the name of God. The Bible refers to God not only as I AM, YHWH, and the Lord but also as Elohim—the plural of El, a generic word for any god—and El Shaddai. After Eve gives birth to Seth, for instance, she says, "God [Elohim] has appointed for me another child," but the next line avers that by the time Seth's son was born, "people began to invoke the name of the LORD [YHWH]" (Genesis 4:25–6). God later explains to Moses, "I appeared to Abraham, Isaac, and Jacob as God Almighty [El Shaddai], but by my name 'The LORD' [YHWH] I did not make myself known to them" (Exodus 6:3). The documentary hypothesis associates each form of God's name with a different version or strand of the narrative, each reflecting a different historical time period and perspective: the J (Jahwist) writer with YHWH, the E (Elohist) writer with Elohim, and the P (Priestly) writer with El Shaddai. In addition, the D (Deuteronomist) writer or writers are associated not only with Deuteronomy but also with Joshua, Judges, Samuel, and Kings. Later, during the Second Temple Period, one or more editors (sometimes called redactors) shaped the J, E, P, and D material into one combined whole.

The documentary hypothesis dominated twentieth-century biblical scholarship and continues to be used and debated today. Broadly speaking, it was the product of a scholarly method known as the Higher Criticism, which developed first in eighteenth-century Germany and rose to prominence among English Bible readers in the nineteenth century. The Higher Criticism implicitly undermined the authority of the Bible as a sacred text by analyzing it according to the same standards that would be applied to any other historical document. Specifically, it took a skeptical view of miracles and aimed to distinguish what was historically verifiable in the Bible from what might be merely legendary. According to this approach, many biblical narratives appeared historically questionable.

If this view of the Bible is accurate, then it seems noteworthy that successive generations of editors did not completely efface earlier material. Instead, they created a mosaic of older and later material. Instead of fashioning one unified narrative, the various editors kept two versions of the creation of humans, two versions of the Ten Commandments, two versions of the rise and fall of the Israelite monarchy, and (much later) four different Gospel accounts of Jesus. What kind of editorial intentions are implied by a text that is less a synthesis or amalgam than a collage or mosaic?

This question returns us to the theoretical issues outlined in the introduction concerning authorial intention. You can quickly see how the question of intentionality becomes extraordinarily complex with the Bible, in which a particular text may involve multiple authors, editors, and translators. What is gained, and what lost, if we assume one implied author when reading such a text? The extensive intertextuality of the Bible further complicates this tension between reading it as a unified whole and reading it as a collage of fragments: it can seem to invite a sense of intentional unity because so many biblical texts explicitly or implicitly allude to other biblical texts. Such intertextual repetitions can appear to support the assumption that we may use one part of the Bible to help interpret another.

Ironically, however, the original poststructuralist definition of *intertextuality* stressed something far more like the modern view of the Bible as a mosaic of textual fragments. As explained in the introduction, if you accept the argument that any interpretation depends on intertextual citations and repetitions, then you recognize the contingency of all interpretations because you recognize the extent to which all interpretations depend on their contexts. After all, changing contexts lead to changing interpretations, as history shows. Indeed, the Bible could be considered a paradigmatic text for poststructuralists. Not only are its component parts highly intertextual (or in*tra*textual, if you read it as a unified text), but also its vast influence on Western cultural history means it has a uniquely extensive intertextual relationship with that history. It is an epicenter of intertextuality.

THE BIBLE AS MODERN

One effect of the Higher Criticism is that it made the Bible appear surprisingly relevant to modern literature. During the early decades of the twentieth century when artists were embracing collage as a distinctively modern art form, readers informed by the Higher Criticism could see the Bible itself as a collage. T. S. Eliot's *The Waste Land* (1922) and William Faulkner's *The Sound and the Fury* (1929) exemplify how modernist literary experiments with collage-like fragmentation effects could find inspiration in the Bible. In these works, the speakers or characters wrestle with a sense of despair represented as the fragmentation of a traditional worldview that once meant something but now cannot be put back together into a coherent or compelling picture. Eliot and Faulkner use biblical allusions to help represent this sense of tradition as incoherent collage.

Modernism was a broad and varied artistic movement in the first half of the twentieth century that sought to break with traditional forms of expression in favor of new artistic forms. In literature, these new forms tended to represent human selfhood or subjectivity as fragmented and riddled with uncertainty. Postmodernism developed in the second half of the twentieth century and is arguably even more varied than modernism. Whereas modernist literature typically represents subjective uncertainty and fragmentation as a problem or even a crisis, postmodern literature typically offers a less anguished and more playful view, embracing intertextuality, irony, and existential possibility.

For many postmodern authors, by contrast, the Bible-as-collage becomes something to play with and even reclaim in new ways. In Tony Kushner's *Angels in America* (1991/92), for example, a character named Prior calls on the Bible as "scriptural precedent" for his own wrestling bout with a powerful angel. Quoting the King James version, he cries, "I will not let thee go except thou bless me!" In a modernist text, his efforts would most likely come to nothing; in *Angels in America*, however, he succeeds in winning the angel's blessing. At the end of the play, Prior blesses the audience itself, breaking the fourth wall as if to pass on the angel's blessing. The play suggests that a theatrical performance in the contemporary world might serve much the same function that sacred stories once did—even as the play also winks at us from behind the curtain, so to speak, leaving us to wrestle with the tension between skepticism and faith.

Salman Rushdie similarly embraces a postmodern sense of subjective uncertainty and possibility in *Midnight's Children* (1981). Rushdie invokes the Bible to help convey a sense of the lush cultural fusions and tensions in modern India. The protagonist's grandfather, Aadam Aziz, resonates with the Garden of Eden story (which is claimed by Jewish, Christian, and Islamic traditions, as the novel implicitly reminds the reader) not only in his name but also because he lives in the Edenic valley of Kashmir. Yet as Indira Karamcheti argues, the novel also undermines the potential authority of this biblical allusion by treating it with comic irreverence and by intertwining it with allusions to a fairy tale, Snow White. Rushdie subtly subverts the pretensions of Western imperialism in that various fragments from the Bible, which has historically been associated with the British colonization of India, are merely a minor set of currents in the complex sea of stories that constitutes the history of modern India. (I borrow this oceanic metaphor for intertextuality from Rushdie's 1990 novel, *Haroun and the Sea of Stories*.)

If the Bible is just a collage of disconnected fragments, then it seems not to be one overarching story at all. As for its component parts, the original forms and contexts of the various stories that make up the collage are largely unrecoverable. As such an untellable tale, the Bible has proved surprisingly relevant to modernist and postmodernist literary works—which, after all, typically imply that *any* story is merely a collage. Indeed, even in such works that play with or fully embrace meaninglessness, one regularly finds a biblically-infused sense of mystery.

SUMMARY

- The Bible narrates the history of the rise and fall of Israel. Christians see Jesus as restoring the fallen Israelite kingdom but in a spiritual way that will be fully realized only at the end of history. *Israel* is an appropriate name for God's chosen nation because people struggle to achieve the ideal (in both the Old and New Testaments). This understanding of the Bible has influenced utopian and dystopian literature as well as less extreme literary representations of the aspirations and failures of governments.
- The Bible chronicles God's interactions with human beings (especially Israel). The stories are meant to reveal the character of God to humans, but they often represent God as transcending ordinary human experience and understanding. The imagery used in these representations has especially influenced literary works that aim to articulate profound and visionary truths.
- The Bible is an edited compilation of texts not originally designed to fit together into a unified whole. These texts suggest a variety of different aims and even worldviews. The Bible is thus a collage of disparate fragments from original sources that remain largely unrecoverable. This modern view of the Bible has resonated powerfully with modernist and postmodernist authors.

QUESTIONS FOR DISCUSSION

1   In your view, who wrote the Bible? What were their aims?
2   What do you think is the most interesting image the Bible uses to represent God as transcendent? Why?
3   Are there aspects of human experience so mysterious that they are difficult to describe? If so, do you think a sense of mystery in a work of imaginative literature can represent such experiential mysteries? Are there other reasons why a sense of mystery in a work of literature might be valuable?
4   What symbols or images might an author use to represent a person, situation, or idea that is only partially knowable? If you wanted to create that kind of representation in your own work of art, what symbol or image might you use?
5   What kinds of literary mysteries do you most enjoy? Do you prefer solvable mysteries such as those typically found in crime novels? Or do you like unsolvable mysteries—those that leave you wondering, or those that feel like an invitation to become a co-creator by "filling in the blanks" left by the artist? Alternatively, do unsolvable mysteries often feel to you like a cheap gimmick?

SUGGESTIONS FOR FURTHER READING

Consider reading one or more of the literary and biblical texts mentioned above. For relevant Bible readings in addition to those mentioned in this chapter, you might begin by exploring Genesis and Exodus. Their stories are essential to acquiring a sense of how the Bible works when read as a unified narrative. For additional literary readings, try Gerard Manley Hopkins's "God's Grandeur" (1877) or Wallace Stevens's "Sunday Morning" (1923).

For relevant nonfiction works, consider the following:

Jones, Norman W. "Faulkner and the Bible: A Haunted Voice." *Critical Insights: William Faulkner.* Ed. Kathryn Artuso. Ipswich, MA: Salem Press, 2013. 202–21. This essay focuses on Faulkner's uses of the Bible, especially in *The Sound and the Fury* and *Absalom, Absalom!*

Karamcheti, Indira. "Salman Rushdie's *Midnight's Children* and an Alternate Genesis." *Pacific Coast Philology* 21.1/2 (November 1986): 81–4. Karamcheti articulates a postcolonial reading of Rushdie's biblical allusions.

Kreitzer, Larry J. *Gospel Images in Fiction and Film: On Reversing the Hermeneutical Flow*. London: Sheffield Academic Press, 2002. Kreitzer analyzes biblical allusions in Conrad's *The Heart of Darkness* and Atwood's *The Handmaid's Tale*. For more on Conrad, see Dwight H. Purdy, *Joseph Conrad's Bible*. Norman: University of Oklahoma Press, 1984.

Prickett, Stephen. *Origins of Narrative: The Romantic Appropriation of the Bible*. Cambridge: Cambridge University Press, 1996. Prickett argues that the Bible began to be read as a novel in the eighteenth and nineteenth centuries, and that it became during this period a model and standard for imaginative literature. For more on the Bible in Romantic English poetry, see also Bryan Shelley, *Shelley and Scripture: The Interpreting Angel*. Oxford: Oxford University Press, 1994; David Jasper, *The Sacred and Secular Canon in Romanticism: Preserving the Sacred Truths*. New York: St. Martin's Press, 1999; Deeanne Westbrook, *Wordsworth's Biblical Ghosts*. New York: Palgrave, 2001; and Adam Potkay, "Romantic Transformations of the King James Bible" in *The King James Bible after 400 Years*, ed. Hannibal Hamlin and Norman W. Jones. Cambridge: Cambridge University Press, 2010: 219–33.

2

FRIENDS, FAMILY, AND LOVERS: A FAMILIAR GOD

If many biblical texts insist that God is beyond human comprehension, then how can the Bible tell readers anything about God? As this chapter shows, certain biblical texts implicitly answer this question by suggesting that the most important clue to the mystery of God is to be found in our relationships with other people. Alongside all the miraculous and sometimes paradoxical imagery used to represent God's transcendence (described in Chapter 1), the Bible also regularly depicts God using the familiar and even ordinary imagery of intimate human relationships—as a friend, a father, and a husband.

The Bible casts God as the friend of Abraham and Moses, the father of Jesus (as well as the adopted father of all who believe in Jesus), and the lover and husband of Israel. In the New Testament, God becomes the lover and fiancé of Christians, too. The New Testament closes by repeating this wedding imagery: when Christ returns, Jerusalem will be Christ's "bride" (Revelation 21:9). Thus at the end of the Bible, we once again find Israel—represented by its capital city, Jerusalem—at the center of a vision of God's future kingdom as God's betrothed. In short, if God is the central character of the overall biblical narrative (as Chapter 1 explains), then Israel is God's leading lady.

Jesus, according to the Gospel of John, is "the Word" of God—the logos or divine reason—who "became flesh and lived among us". (John 1:14)

This bride-and-groom metaphor represents what has traditionally come to be described as God's immanence—God as not wholly separate from the material world but existing within it in ways that are accessible to human understanding and experience, at least to a significant extent. Christians emphasize this immanence of God in the person of Jesus. Post-biblical Christian theology describes Jesus as God *incarnate* (literally God *made flesh*), both God and human in one person. In Hebrew scripture, the immanence of God may be found in the ark of the covenant and the temple but also in the history of God's interactions with the Israelites—the history recounted in Hebrew scripture itself. Deuteronomy 30:11–13 insists, "the word" of God is "not in heaven" or "beyond the sea" but is "very near to you." It is in the commandments given to Moses and, more broadly, in the Torah, the five books of Moses. According to Deuteronomy 30, the word of God may thereby be found "in your mouth and in your heart for you to observe." In Rabbinic Judaism, which developed after the Second Temple was destroyed, the presence of God—the *Shekinah*, in Hebrew—may be experienced wherever Torah is faithfully read and studied.

Before we get too comfortable with the idea that God is immanent, however, we should remember how frequently the biblical texts insist that God also remains a mystery to a significant extent. Even when using familiar, non-supernatural imagery for God, the Bible (read as a whole) does not limit itself to just one metaphor—friend, father, husband—but instead uses all three. This can serve to remind us that these are metaphors: they are not literal but figurative ways of representing God indirectly. After all, according to traditional Judeo-Christian beliefs, God cannot be represented directly (as discussed in Chapter 1). For some readers, these multiple metaphors suggest that biblical texts differ from and even contradict one another. This returns us to the initial question: how can the Bible represent an unrepresentable being? In addition, what does all this have to do with literature?

SOME BACKGROUND: CHANGING HISTORICAL CONTEXTS

Many literary authors of widely varying worldviews—secular and religious alike—have been inspired by biblical stories about human relationships. I suspect this is in part because these stories are too juicy to resist: they are rich with the complexity of human frailties. My students are often shocked (and delighted!) to find that people in the Bible behave so badly. The wide-ranging influence of these stories also derives from their implicit suggestion that our relationships with other people are vitally and profoundly important. Indeed, some suggest that human relationships constitute one of the ways we come to know God. Even secular authors have felt attracted to this idea, sometimes seeing it as a metaphorical articulation of the ways in which intimate relationships can occasion insights that are not necessarily divine but are nonetheless profound—inspiring, or shattering, or sometimes both at once.

Plato's *Symposium* (c. 385–370 BCE) also suggests a sense of profundity in intimate relationships, especially those in which we find ourselves attracted by another person's exceptional beauty or goodness. Such attractions inevitably end in disappointment, according to the traditional reading of Plato, because the true object of such desires is not a person but the pure "forms" or ideals of Beauty and Goodness. These forms can be reflected in a person but actually exist beyond material reality, so they are perceived most clearly through a kind of intellectual vision. Socrates, a character in Plato's *Symposium*, recounts how a wise woman named Diotima taught him that human experiences of love can lead from the "lowest," most lustful type of love to the "highest," most intellectual type (hence the notion of Platonic love), whose ultimate object is not a person but the abstract form of Beauty, Goodness, and even Divinity.

Platonism or Neoplatonism (Platonic thought influenced by the third-century CE philosopher Plotinus) plays an important role in biblical reception history, from early Christian theologians such as Augustine of Hippo (in the fourth and fifth centuries CE) to later ones such as Thomas Aquinas (in the thirteenth century CE) and beyond. Augustine, for example, famously contends that erotic desires are actually confused expressions of a deep and often unrecognized need for God's love. Yet this Neoplatonic aspect of biblical reception history can obscure important differences between Neoplatonic conceptions of God and biblical portrayals of God—differences that have arguably become clearer in recent centuries than they were to Christian theologians a thousand years ago.

In Hebrew scripture, God is generally not presented as an idea, proposition, or abstract truth like the Platonic forms of Goodness, Truth, or Beauty, which are unchanging, unmoved by emotion, and only indirectly and dimly evident in the material world. It was Neoplatonism that helped create the now-familiar image of disembodied souls of faithful Christians rising up to an ethereal heaven after they die. The Bible, by contrast, offers rather different images of the afterlife. The Old Testament does not emphasize the afterlife, although it does regularly refer to *Sheol*, which ancient scholars aptly translated as *Hades: Sheol* seems quite similar to the underworld of shades in Greek mythology (e.g., Job 7:9). The New Testament generally suggests an embodied afterlife here on earth, which will begin only at the end of history when the kingdom of God descends from heaven to restore the world to an Eden-like state. In keeping with this embodied, concrete (as opposed to abstract) imagery, the Bible tends to depict God not as an idea but as a character in the stories it tells. He takes action, redirects human history, forms special relationships with certain people and groups, and sometimes even seems to have his desires thwarted. In short, God is like a person (indeed, orthodox Christian theology understands God as three persons in one).

To put it in more biblical terms, people are like God. After all, God makes humans in his "image" (Genesis 1:26). We are not told precisely how humans are like God, but the Gospel of Matthew helps reinforce what later came to be known as the *imago dei* doctrine (Latin for "the image of God"): Jesus insists that helping a person in need is the same as helping him (Matthew 25:40). Indeed, Jesus distills all of scripture—"the law and the prophets"—in a way that reinforces this idea that our relationships with other people reflect our relationship with God: "You shall love the Lord your God with all your heart, and with all your soul, and with all your mind," he explains, calling this "the greatest and first commandment" and then noting that a second commandment "is like it," as if made in the image of the first: "You shall love your neighbor as yourself" (Matthew 22:34–40). Indeed, earlier in the same Gospel,

Jesus uses this "second" commandment by itself as the distillation of all scripture: "Do to others as you would have them do to you; for this is the law and the prophets" (Matthew 7:12). Romans 13 and Galatians 5 likewise emphasize this point: "the whole law is summed up in a single commandment, 'You shall love your neighbor as yourself'" (Galatians 5:14).

These New Testament passages quote the Old Testament: "You shall not take vengeance or bear a grudge against any of your people, but you shall love your neighbor as yourself" (Leviticus 19:18). This key point of connection between Old and New belies a long-standing misinterpretation of the New Testament as a radical reversal of the Old Testament. According to this view, which derives especially from Augustine's reading of Paul's New Testament epistles, the New Testament emphasizes God's loving mercy whereas the Old Testament emphasizes a mercilessly legalistic sense of justice. While this interpretation is part of the Bible's reception history (witness Shakespeare's *Merchant of Venice*, c.1596), it can encourage anti-Semitism and does not accurately represent traditional Jewish interpretations of Hebrew scripture.

It is true that the Sermon on the Mount contrasts the Mosaic laws with the teachings of Jesus: "You have heard that it was said, 'An eye for an eye and a tooth for a tooth.' But I say to you, do not resist an evildoer. But if anyone strikes you on the right cheek, turn the other also" (Matthew 5). Yet this is not so much a reversal as an extension of Old Testament teachings, emphasizing an ideal articulated in passages such as Proverbs 20:22 ("Do not say, 'I will repay evil'; wait for the LORD, and he will help you") and Isaiah 50:6 ("I gave my back to those who struck me, and my cheeks to those who pulled out the beard"). This is arguably an impossible ideal, which many (most famously the sixteenth-century theologian Martin Luther) have interpreted as pointing to the need for God's love and forgiveness, or in Christian parlance, God's grace. Old Testament laws similarly promote *chesed*, a transliteration of the Hebrew term for loving kindness and mercy. These laws were at least somewhat more compassionate and equitable than other legal codes of their time: "an eye for an eye" and other such rules commended not vindictive punishment but a measure of restraint from excessive retributive vengeance.

Indeed, Exodus 23 exhorts the Israelites not only to care for non-Israelites and the poor but also their enemies: "When you come upon your enemy's ox or donkey going astray, you shall bring it back." Similarly, Leviticus 19:9–18 charges Israel with caring for those who are deaf, blind, or poor, and it reminds the Israelites that they should love foreigners as they love themselves. According to Deuteronomy 15, all outstanding debts must be forgiven every seven years, and Leviticus 25 establishes a Jubilee Sabbath of Sabbaths in which debts will be forgiven every forty-ninth (seven times seven) or fiftieth year. Elsewhere, Hebrew scripture insists that God desires not animal sacrifices but justice and mercy (1 Samuel 15:22, Psalm 51:16–17, Proverbs 21:3, Hosea 6:6, and Amos 5:21–4).

If one reads the Ten Commandments or Decalogue (meaning *Ten Words*) in this light, they fall neatly into two complementary halves (see Exodus 20). The first four or so (different traditions count them differently) focus on the Israelites' relationship with God. The remaining six focus on relationships between people. In keeping with the traditional interpretation of the Sermon on the Mount as pointing to the need for God's love (noted above), it is also worth pointing out that according to Jewish traditions, the Ten Commandments and the other laws of Moses enshrine *chesed* in more ways than are sometimes recognized: the commandments are considered blessings, *mitzvot* (the plural of *mitzvah*), because they are signs that the Israelites are loved by God and chosen to be a holy nation. A more accurate modern translation of "law" in the Bible might therefore be "instruction." The people obey these instructions not in order to avoid punishment or earn God's love but because they are already loved, chosen to be God's bride, children, or friends. "Righteous" people therefore take "delight" in the law (Psalm 1).

FRIENDSHIP IN THE BIBLE: A MATTER OF TRUST

This sense of already being loved by God helps explain why the Ten Commandments begin by reminding the Israelites that God rescued them from oppression—reminding them that they have already been chosen: "I am the LORD your God, who brought you out of the land of Egypt, out of the house of slavery" (Exodus 20). This is similar to ancient Mesopotamian vassal treaties in which a superior party would agree to provide protection and other favors toward an inferior party in exchange for loyalty: the opening would recount how the superior party had provided protection in the past as a way of offering evidence that the promises made in this new treaty could be fulfilled. This is to say, the covenant with Moses and the Israelites follows a model that implicitly casts God in the role of a king, in keeping with one of the primary metaphors used for God through-out the Bible. It also emphasizes the importance of trust—that the Israelites can trust God.

The Mosaic covenant is trustworthy because it fulfills and elabo-rates on earlier covenants recounted in Hebrew scripture, especially the covenant with Abraham. In return for Abraham's loyalty, God promises to provide a fertile homeland and countless descendants. This promise is similar to ancient "royal grant" treaties, a simpler agreement than vassal treaties, which usually granted land in return for loyalty. Abraham and his male descendants must show their loy-alty by being circumcised. Today such circumcisions are performed in a ceremony called a *bris*, an eastern European pronunciation of the Hebrew *berit*, which means covenant. Ultimately, the biblical story of Israel as a people is the story of God's fulfillment of this original covenant with Abraham.

That story includes other covenants, such as God's covenant with Noah after the great flood, in which the rainbow serves as the sign that God will never again destroy so many of his creatures. Much later, as Israel grows into a powerful kingdom, God promises David that his descendants will rule forever. The Gospels emphasize that Jesus is descended from David because Christians interpret Jesus as fulfilling the Davidic covenant. Jesus also fulfills the earlier bibli-cal covenants, as well, in a new covenant or New Testament—the Greek word usually translated as *testament* may also be translated *covenant*.

These stories should help remind us that it would be wise to pause before we leap to twenty-first-century conclusions about what the

I will make your offspring as numerous as the stars of heaven, and will give to your offspring all these lands. (Genesis 26:4)

Bible means when it describes God as a friend, father, or husband. These terms have a long history that attests to important changes in how people in different times and cultures thought about such relationships. For example, the Bible does not emphasize equality as an ideal for human relationships as much as it emphasizes trust. Every time the Bible describes God as the "God of Abraham" or the "God of Abraham, Isaac, and Jacob" (see, for example, Genesis 28:13, Exodus 3, 1 Kings 18:36, Matthew 22:32, and Acts 3:13), it implicitly invokes God's covenants and suggests that he can be trusted based on the promises he has fulfilled in the past.

Consider the story of Adam and Eve in this light. The opening of Genesis introduces us to its main character by suggesting that God, among other things, creates the world as an orderly and good place in which humans are important: they are created in God's image and serve as vice-regents, if you will, over God's creation. (By contrast, the Mesopotamian account of creation, the *Enuma Elish*, depicts a chaotic world in which human beings are created to serve violent gods.) As with his later covenants, God requires a sign of loyalty in return: Adam and Eve are forbidden to eat from the tree of the knowledge of good and evil (Genesis 2).

How does the serpent convince Eve to disobey God? He casts doubt on the story Eve has believed until then: he tells an alternative story that casts God not as trustworthy and powerful but as deceptive and vulnerable to having his power usurped. The serpent avers, "God knows that when you eat" the forbidden fruit, "your eyes will be opened, and you will be like God, knowing good and evil" (Genesis 3). The serpent's argument is not really about eating the fruit but about doubting Adam and Eve's relationship with God, specifically doubting that they can trust God.

As it turns out, the serpent is the untrustworthy one. He is partly right: Adam and Eve do learn about good and evil, although not in a way that makes them god-like. Quite the opposite. They learn what it means not to trust God, to reject their covenantal relationship with God, which leaves them feeling so far from powerful that they hide in fear (Genesis 3:10). The meaning of *evil* suggested here entails distrust (the serpent argues that God has not told them the truth), which leads to a sense of unfairness (he implies that God's prohibition is unfair because Adam and Eve should be able to eat the fruit) and jealousy (he plays on Eve's desire to be more powerful).

Many of the subsequent stories told in the Bible may be read as repetitions of this first decision to distrust God. In the story of Cain and Abel, for example, Cain implicitly distrusts God by refusing to heed God's warning. Cain's sense of unfairness then turns to jealousy of his brother, Abel, who has not turned away from God (Genesis 4). God's faithfulness and justice figure prominently in the story. He does not allow Abel's murder to go unpunished; yet in response to Cain's desperate plea for mercy, God puts a mark on Cain to protect him from injustice at the hands of others. Similarly, God makes clothes for Adam and Eve to protect them even though he also punishes them for breaking their covenant.

While both of these stories involve familial relationships, the importance of friendship rises to the fore when we consider God as the central character. After all, both stories focus on breaking the bonds of trust between God and humans—the same kinds of bonds formalized in the stories about God's covenants with Abraham and Moses. "Friendship" might not seem to be the right word to describe relationships between such vastly unequal parties, but this is precisely how the Bible describes them. Abraham was "the friend of God" (James 2:23 and Isaiah 41:8), and "the LORD used to speak to Moses face to face, as one speaks to a friend" (Exodus 33:11). Despite their inequality, God even lets Abraham and Moses win an argument or two with him (Genesis 18 and Exodus 32).

The new covenant in Jesus also embraces friendship. Jesus calls his disciples friends, not servants, foreshadowing his own death as he explains, "No one has greater love than this, to lay down one's life for one's friends" (John 15:13–15). (The Society of Friends, also known as Quakers, takes its name from these verses.) This kind of love—*agape* in the original Greek, as opposed to *eros* (erotic love),

Do not press me to leave you or to turn back from following you! Where you go, I will go; where you lodge, I will lodge; your people shall be my people, and your God my God. (Ruth 1:16)

philia (friendly regard), or *storge* (familial affections)—is famously celebrated by Paul in 1 Corinthians 13:

> If I speak in the tongues of mortals and of angels, but do not have love, I am a noisy gong or a clanging cymbal. And if I have prophetic powers, and understand all mysteries and all knowledge, and if I have all faith, so as to remove mountains, but do not have love, I am nothing. If I give away all my possessions, and if I hand over my body so that I may boast, but do not have love, I gain nothing. Love is patient; love is kind; love is not envious or boastful or arrogant or rude. It does not insist on its own way; it is not irritable or resentful; it does not rejoice in wrongdoing, but rejoices in the truth. It bears all things, believes all things, hopes all things, endures all things.

Paul commends *agape* as the greatest of Christian virtues, more important even than faith itself.

The Bible champions this unselfish form of love in its depictions of the friendships between Ruth and Naomi (in the Book of Ruth) and David and Jonathan (in 1 Samuel 18–23 and 2 Samuel 1). After her husband dies, Ruth would be better off returning to her father's home than staying with her destitute mother-in-law, Naomi. Likewise, when Jonathan's father, King Saul, wants David killed because he fears that David will usurp his authority as king, Jonathan risks his own wellbeing by remaining loyal to David. The biblical accounts of these friendships have inspired not only friendships and wedding ceremonies (especially Ruth's pledge to Naomi) but also, in more recent times, lesbian and gay literature (David famously says of Jonathan in 2 Samuel 1, "your love to me was wonderful, passing the love of women"). Reading these friendships as erotic may reflect anachronistically modern assumptions about the special significance of sex, but such readings have nonetheless played an important role in the modern reception history of the Bible.

The soul of Jonathan was bound to the soul of David, and Jonathan loved him as his own soul. (1 Samuel 18:1)

The story of Adam and Eve clearly addresses sex. It recounts the genesis of sexual shame (they were unashamedly naked before they disobeyed) and gender inequality in marriage (part of Eve's punishment is that her husband will "rule over" her). The story also describes marriage (and implicitly sex) as a physical union whereby husband and wife "become one flesh" because they were originally made from one flesh—Eve made from Adam's rib (Genesis 2–3). Yet the original impetus for the relationship between Adam and Eve is not sexual union or even procreation (despite the Genesis 1:28 injunction to "be fruitful and multiply" in the first account of the creation of men and women) but rather friendship. God says, "It is not good that the man should be alone; I will make him a helper as his partner" (Genesis 2). He tries animals first, but as none of them turns out to be a suitable partner, God creates Eve.

Ecclesiastes seems to reinforce this sense of partnership in a passage that also sometimes appears in wedding ceremonies: "Two are better than one ... For if they fall, one will lift up the other ... And though one might prevail against another, two will withstand one" (Ecclesiastes 4). In 1 Corinthians 12, Paul offers a similar image of the strength created by the unity of believers: they are different from one another but need each other, much like the different parts of the human body. The repeated biblical emphasis on this ideal of unselfish and mutually beneficial relationships influenced post-biblical Christian efforts to explain how God could be Father, Son, and Holy Spirit yet still be one God: God was conceived of as a social or relational being.

Chapter 1 describes how biblical depictions of God's transcendence have influenced literary history through key symbols as well as more generally through the embrace of figurative language. This chapter's focus on biblical representations of God's immanence also highlights figurative language—person, friend, father, lover, husband—but additionally, and perhaps more importantly in terms of literary history, it places storytelling center-stage. To the extent that God may be understood as person-like, or to the extent that we approach God as a character in the Bible, stories become vital because they constitute the primary means by which we typically learn about people and characters.

One of the simplest ways to illustrate this claim is to distinguish strictly factual knowledge from knowledge gained by familiarity.

Certain romance languages (such as French and Spanish) use different verbs for these two ways of knowing: in those languages, you would not say "I know Mary" using the same verb *to know* as you would use in the statement, "I know the square root of 256." While English uses the same verb for both, we do not know a person in the same way that we know the answer to a mathematical problem or a geography question (e.g., what is the tallest mountain in the world?). Knowledge of mathematical equations and factual statements depends on logical proofs and incontrovertible evidence. Knowledge of a person depends on experience, a fuzzier kind of evidence that entails knowing at least part of that person's life story. Even if these two ways of knowing are not mutually exclusive but might best be conceived as two ends of a continuum, there is still a distinction to be made, which may help explain why the Bible primarily tells stories rather than offering philosophical proofs. The Bible depicts God as beyond human comprehension to a significant extent, which would seem to exclude the kind of knowledge one might gain by equations or incontrovertible evidence. It focuses on telling stories, suggesting that God can be known primarily in the fuzzier kinds of ways we use to know other people—narrative ways of knowing that are also the province of imaginative literature (as discussed in the introduction).

FATHERS PLAYING FAVORITES

When read as a unified story, the Bible's use of *father* as a metaphor for God presents more interpretive difficulties than its use of *friend* does, especially if the father metaphor potentially reflects other biblical examples of fatherhood. Consider David, one of the Bible's most famous fathers. While not quite as complex a character as God, David possesses a dizzying variety of qualities: he is beautiful, brave, strong, a talented musician and poet, a skillful warrior, a charismatic lover, a cunning outlaw, a powerful and politically savvy king—savvy perhaps to the point of being manipulative—as well as a deceitful and murderous adulterer. Through it all, the text insists that David trusts God. His story begins in 1 Samuel 16 and runs through 1 Kings 2 (the same story is told with some differences in 1 Chronicles 10 through 29). In addition, David is traditionally thought to have composed much of the Book of Psalms. Some scholars argue that the Bible's varied depiction of this heroic-yet-flawed character must be a composite or collage of fragments from stories about various different Israelite folk-heroes. It can be instructive to try to imagine how the various aspects of David's story might fit into one whole: my students enjoy trying to think of literary characters, movie stars, or politicians who possess a similar range of skills and personality traits.

As a father, David seems no simpler than he does in his other roles. His son, Absalom, kills his half-brother, Amnon, for raping Absalom's sister (2 Samuel 13–19). Estranged from his father as a result, Absalom raises an army to overthrow David. While the story is as dramatic as any modern soap opera, the Bible tells it in a characteristically spare style, using just a few brush strokes to paint strong emotions. After David's soldiers defeat Absalom's, David learns of his son's death:

> The king said to the Cushite, "Is it well with the young man Absalom?" The Cushite answered, "May the enemies of my lord the king, and all who rise up to do you harm, be like that young man." The king was deeply moved, and went up to the chamber over the gate, and wept; and as he went, he said, "O my son Absalom, my son, my son Absalom! Would I had died instead of you."
>
> (2 Samuel 18:32–3)

The Cushite's answer is guardedly indirect, but David understands although he offers no reply. David's lament implies that he would rather have lost the battle than his son, an irony not lost on his soldiers: "Victory that day was turned into mourning for all the troops ... [who] stole into the city that day as soldiers steal in who are ashamed when they flee in battle." The imagery drives home the ironic reversal: they were victorious in battle but now retreat as if in defeat. The story continues to build dramatic tension through another unexpected reversal: not only does the king mourn for the traitor, turning victory into defeat, but also a servant, Joab, corrects his master. Joab warns David that his mourning may turn his own army against him, because it appears that "if Absalom were alive and all of us were dead today, then you would be pleased" (2 Samuel 19). Whether out of political necessity or genuine loyalty to those who risked their lives for him, David stops mourning and celebrates their victory with his soldiers.

The story raises questions but does not provide enough information for definitive answers. What is David's motivation for following Joab's advice? If David loves Absalom that much, then why did he not make amends with him earlier when Absalom sought to end their estrangement? David did not punish Amnon for raping Absalom's sister, Tamar, because David favored Amnon as his firstborn son (by a different mother than that of Absalom and Tamar). Does David later regret how he handled this series of tragedies among his children?

The story of David and Absalom is typical of biblical narratives in that it does not provide the detailed accounts of thoughts and emotions that modern readers generally expect. At the same time, however, these narratives do provide psychological details and drama. Yet you must look carefully to see them, and they invariably cast mysterious shadows even as they provide flashes of illumination. As Robert Alter argues, biblical narratives thus create a sense of mystery about human motivation—a sense of doubt about our ability to know other people surely or completely.

It follows, then, that in exploring the Bible's anthropomorphic depictions of God's immanence—of God as a character or person—we should not assume that we will find easy or simple characterizations. Indeed, God's immanence may be no less mysterious than his transcendence. The Bible's reception history shows that it is easier for some people to imagine God as a transcendent, otherworldly being than as a friend, father, or lover—perhaps because we know only too well how those familiar relationships can be anything but clear or simple.

An even more famous biblical father-son story exemplifies this complexity. Often referred to as "the prodigal son," this New Testament parable follows an irresponsible young man who squanders his inheritance in "wild living," eventually finding himself impoverished and starving (Luke 15). He decides to return home and beg for help from his father. On the way, he rehearses his plea: he is no longer worthy to be his father's son and so will beg to be hired as a servant. Yet the father sees him coming and runs to embrace him even before he makes his speech. The father then throws a party to celebrate, which rankles the young man's older and more responsible brother: he complains that no celebration has ever been thrown for him, despite that he has worked "like a slave."

The father explains, "Son, you are always with me, and all that is mine is yours. But we had to celebrate and rejoice, because this brother of yours was dead and has come to life; he was lost and has been found" (Luke 15:31).

As a parable, this story invites an allegorical interpretation according to which every major element of the story carries a figurative meaning. Traditional readings view the father as God. The prodigal son may represent Jewish sinners of Jesus' day whereas the good son represents Jews who obey God's laws. Or the prodigal son may represent Gentile converts (non-Jews who joined the early followers of Jesus in increasing numbers) whereas the good son represents the Jewish inheritors of the promise to Abraham. The New Testament attests to tensions between these two groups. Or the prodigal son may represent you, the reader, if you identify with that character. Or the good son may represent you if you identify with him. The story has often been read in this kind of personal, self-reflective way. Or you may read it as inviting all three sets of possibilities at once, in ways that overlap (is it possible to identify with both brothers in different ways?).

What about the father—what kind of person is he? Interestingly, he gives half of his estate to his irresponsible son and later implicitly trusts that same son even before he hears an explanation or apology. (My students usually do not trust the prodigal as much as the father does.) Both sons underestimate or misunderstand their father's love. Yet is it really okay for someone simply to repent and be entirely forgiven without being required to make amends? How do we know the prodigal son truly repents? If we generalize the story by extending its implications to those who commit even more hurtful misdeeds, then might the good son have a better reason to object? Should the father have done more to guide his irresponsible son, including not giving him such a large fortune so young? Such questions are just the beginning. This parable has a rich reception history that bears witness to the fact that most biblical parables can be interpreted in many different ways (much like the Bible itself!). That can be frustrating, and some conclude that these texts are ultimately incoherent. Others recall the parable Nathan tells David about the rich man who took advantage of a poor man (discussed in the introduction), and they explore these texts as interactive tools for self-reflection.

> Consider the lilies of the field, how they grow; they neither toil nor spin, yet I tell you, even Solomon in all his glory was not clothed like one of these. But if God so clothes the grass of the field, which is alive today and tomorrow is thrown into the oven, will he not much more clothe you—you of little faith? (Matthew 6)

The prodigal's father has traditionally been taken to represent God not only because many of Jesus' parables focus on God but also because he frequently refers to God as *father*—and not only as his own. "Call no one your father on earth, for you have one Father—the one in heaven" (Matthew 23:9). Likewise, Jesus promises his followers new brothers, sisters, and mothers, implying that God is their new father (Mark 3:31–5 and 10:28–30). This is the origin of the long Christian tradition of referring to fellow believers as *brother* and *sister*, evident in a variety of contexts from monasteries and convents to African American literature and culture. You find *father* used as a metaphor for God more often in the New Testament than in Hebrew scripture, but you do find it there, too (examples include Exodus 4:22–3, Deuteronomy 32:6, Psalm 89:26, and Isaiah 63:16).

As with the biblical portrayals of great friendships, its depictions of God-as-father tend to invoke the ideal of a love that is neither self-interested nor self-serving. Jesus keeps trying to convince people that they can trust God more than they realize.

At the same time, however, you may find unsettling tensions in the Bible's use of this parent-and-child metaphor for God—as suggested by the David-and-Absalom story, in which David favors one child over another and seems to regret, in the end, the way he enforced justice on Absalom. Again and again, biblical stories seem to emphasize the strife and suffering caused by parents who play favorites with their children. Isaac favors Esau while Rebekah favors Jacob, which creates discord between the twins and their parents such that Jacob is eventually forced to leave (Genesis 25–8). Jacob, in turn, favors Joseph over his other sons, which makes Joseph's brothers so jealous that they sell him into slavery (Genesis 37). These two stories ultimately suggest that the less-favored children also have good fortune, but other biblical stories about sibling rivalries focus the reader's attention on the pain of the less-favored—Ishmael's plight when his half-brother, Isaac, is favored (Genesis 21), or Leah's anguish when her more beautiful sister, Rachel, wins Jacob's heart (Genesis 29–30). In both cases, God comforts those not chosen.

Yet God also plays favorites, most of all in choosing Israel over other peoples but also in choosing David over his older brothers (1 Samuel 16) and Moses over other Israelite leaders (Numbers 12). Similarly, the New Testament describes the chief priests as jealous of Jesus (Mark 15:10). Twentieth-century Swiss theologian Karl Barth argued that God ultimately favors all because those not initially chosen get blessed by those who are chosen. Abraham is chosen, for example, and many interpret Genesis 18:18 as promising that "all the nations of the earth shall be blessed in him." Joseph's brothers are saved by Joseph when famine strikes. Jesus is chosen, and while some Christians believe that only the faithful are blessed through his death and resurrection, others believe that all people are thus blessed (based on passages such as 2 Corinthians 5:15 and 1 John 2:2).

Perhaps it makes sense in this light that the Bible sometimes casts sibling jealousy as a missed opportunity. Martha resents her sister, Mary, for idly listening to Jesus while Martha works hard to prepare for their guest. When Martha asks for help, Jesus rebukes her: "Martha, you are worried and distracted by many things; there is need of only one thing. Mary has chosen the better part, which will not be taken away from her" (Luke 10). Many of us (especially those of us who identify with Martha's hard work!) wonder whether this rebuke is entirely fair. Yet like the older brother in the prodigal son parable—and arguably also like Cain and Esau—maybe Martha has misunderstood something important.

Such stories might suggest that God chooses one person over another based on merit: Israel, Moses, David, and Mary deserve to be favored. If so, however, then it remains unclear how such merit gets determined. After all, Israel, Moses, and David fail God at times (Israel fails repeatedly; regarding Moses, see Numbers 20). Similarly, Jesus chooses Peter as a leader despite that Peter misunderstands and abandons Jesus (Mark 8:27–33 and 14:29–72). He chooses Paul, too, despite that Paul at first persecutes Jesus' followers (Acts 7:58–9:31). The Bible at times acknowledges the mysteriousness of these choices, as when God explains to Samuel, "the LORD does not see as mortals see; they look on the outward appearance, but the LORD looks on the heart" (1 Samuel 16:7). Yet this does not fully dispel the mystery, as it reinforces the sense that humans cannot understand God's choices.

The Bible's depictions of God as a father potentially evoke even more disturbing stories, such as when Lot offers his virgin daughters to be raped by the men of Sodom (Genesis 19). Does the story condone this offer? Jephthah makes a reckless vow that forces him to sacrifice his own daughter (Judges 11). Saul tries to murder his son, Jonathan (1 Samuel 20). The Bible's reception history testifies to recurring questions about the potentially sexist and even misogynist implications of God being cast as a father, especially given the patriarchal cultural context of biblical stories about fathers. Perhaps motivated in part by such questions, there has been a longstanding interest in the maternal aspects of God. The prophet Isaiah speaks with the voice of God, saying, "as a mother comforts her child, so I will comfort you" (Isaiah 66:12–13). Fourteenth-century writer Julian of Norwich celebrates God as both father and mother: "God rejoices that he is our Father, and God rejoices that he is our Mother."

A JEALOUS LOVER

The problem of favoritism and jealousy in families becomes even more pointed when it comes to the Bible's metaphorical representations of God as a lover and husband. God is "a jealous God," according to the Ten Commandments, and when the Israelites worship other gods, it is like committing adultery in the most degrading way: they "lusted after other gods" (Judges 2:17), "committed lewdness" (Ezekiel 16:43), and "played the whore" (Hosea 4:12). The prophet Jeremiah accuses Israel of having sex with "many lovers" so openly and frequently that he caustically demands, "Where have you not been lain with?" (Jeremiah 3:2). These metaphorical descriptions of worshiping other gods promote a visceral sense of intimate betrayal, violation, and degradation.

One can easily imagine how this sordid imagery has lent itself to Christian traditions that view sex in largely negative ways. Influenced by ancient Greek Stoicism, these traditions cast sex as

> Set me as a seal upon your heart, as a seal upon your arm;
> for love is strong as death, passion fierce as the grave. Its
> flashes are flashes of fire, a raging flame. Many waters can-
> not quench love, neither can floods drown it. If one offered
> for love all the wealth of one's house, it would be utterly
> scorned. (Song of Solomon 8)

the product of base, animalistic desires whose only rational outlet is for procreation. The image of Israel as wife and God as husband, which gets repeated in the New Testament's figuring of Jesus as the bridegroom (Matthew 9:15) and the heavenly city of Jerusalem as the bride (Revelation 21), can also reinforce patriarchal values whereby "the husband is the head of the wife" (Ephesians 5:23). The Bible's reception history certainly attests to the prevalence of such values.

Yet the Bible also strikes other notes in its depictions of sex and romance. The writings of Paul commend celibacy but also encourage spouses not to deprive each other of sexual pleasure except by mutual agreement "for a set time, to devote yourselves to prayer, and then come together again" (1 Corinthians 7:5). Paul makes no mention of procreation to justify sex; only pleasure. In keeping with the Bible's celebrations of unselfish friendships, Paul offers an egalitarian image of a married couple enjoying each other's bodies: "the wife does not have authority over her own body, but the husband does; likewise the husband does not have authority over his own body, but the wife does" (1 Corinthians 7:4).

Arguably the most famous biblical depiction of romantic love is found in the Song of Solomon, which reads like a play in which a young woman and a young man profess their love for each other in unabashedly physical terms. They take turns, the young woman going first, each describing the other's body in ways that at times seem strangely and even amusingly archaic to my students but that clearly celebrate erotic desire. This short book has traditionally been interpreted as an allegorical expression of the love between God and the faithful. While it might be tempting to dismiss such a reading as a prudish cover-up, the closing notes of the drama (see inset) articulate a poetic sense of the power and vitality of romantic love that indeed gestures toward transcendence.

LOVE AS MIRACULOUS

In Geoffrey Chaucer's fourteenth-century *The Canterbury Tales*, the Wife of Bath questions the negative attitudes about sex promoted by early Christian theologians such as Augustine and Jerome. To appreciate the richness of her argument, consider the context. A diverse assortment of characters travel together on a pilgrimage to the shrine of St Thomas Becket at Canterbury Cathedral. Along the way, they engage in a storytelling contest. This pilgrimage story serves as the frame narrative for all of the characters' stories in the sense that it frames or establishes the context in which each story gets told. Further emphasizing this larger context, some characters' stories begin with a prologue that tells us something about the storyteller. This frame-narrative structure, found in other medieval texts such as *The Thousand and One Nights* (often known in English as *The Arabian Nights*) and Giovanni Boccaccio's *The Decameron*, can render even apparently simple tales more complex and interesting by inviting the reader to consider how each individual tale reflects on the larger frame narrative, potentially illuminating the storyteller's perspective, motivations, and relationships with the other characters. When it comes to the Bible, attention to frame narratives can help remind us of the danger of interpreting brief passages out of context: their original contexts help us understand what such passages mean. Change the context, and the meaning changes.

The Wife of Bath's tale recounts a battle of the sexes, so to speak. A knight is condemned to death for rape, but his life will be spared if he can discover what women desire most. His quest is fruitless until the very end when an enchantress reveals to him that women wish to have authority over their husbands. In exchange for this answer, the knight must marry her; furthermore, he must choose whether she will be ugly but faithful or beautiful but unfaithful. Stymied by this choice, the knight asks the enchantress to choose for herself—which is exactly what she wants, in keeping with the answer to his quest. So the enchantress becomes both beautiful and faithful, and the two live happily ever after.

In short, the man gets what he wants only when he lets the woman get what she wants. In the context of the frame narrative (especially her prologue, which includes an extensive argument about the Bible's teachings on marriage), the Wife of Bath's tale resonates with Paul's ideal of husband and wife giving their bodies to each other sexually in what might be described as a mutual self-dispossession (discussed above). Only when both spouses prioritize the other's desire are their own desires fulfilled.

Yet the Wife's prologue further suggests that her story is not just about sex and marriage: it is also about interpreting the Bible. In an ironically offhand way, she demonstrates a thorough knowledge of relevant biblical passages as she argues against the prevailing authorities of her day—the "men" who "conjecture and interpret up and down"—who teach that celibacy is more virtuous than marriage and that a woman should be married to only one man. "God commanded us to grow fruitful and multiply; that gentle text I can well understand," she avers. Citing the practice of polygamy in the Bible, she wishes she could follow King Solomon's example, who had a thousand wives and concubines: "would God it were lawful to me to be refreshed half so often as he!"

By casting men as the opposition in her interpretive debate about the Bible, the Wife of Bath's prologue stages an interpretive battle of the sexes that potentially mirrors the battle of the sexes described in her tale about the knight, thus implying that the same solution might resolve both battles. That is to say, she suggests a more generous and other-oriented approach to interpreting the Bible. After all, she argues, more than one interpretation is possible: the Bible offers different examples we might follow when it comes to sex and marriage. Paul seems to promote such a generous interpretive approach in Romans (especially chapters 14 and 15), where he insists that we should think of others rather than ourselves when we try to interpret how to apply scriptural codes of conduct. He warns against judging others, which echoes Jesus's words in the Gospels: "Do not judge, so that you may not be judged. For with the judgment you make you will be judged" (Matthew 7:1–2; see also the parable of the unforgiving servant in Matthew 18). Much as David found himself judged by his own judgment of Nathan's parable, the Bible as a whole can serve as a parable-like tool for self-reflection in this regard. Some critics have charged the Wife of Bath with citing scripture too selectively, but so do her male opponents. Chaucer arguably uses her prologue and tale to suggest a generous, non-judgmental model for how to interpret the Bible within a Christian community—a model derived from Paul's *agape*-oriented vision of loving your spouse as yourself in a Christian marriage.

While many authors have been inspired by Paul's ideal of marriage as embodying mutual self-dispossession and trust, many have also represented the failure to achieve this ideal as utterly devastating. Several influential examples of modernist literature describe failed attempts to achieve an ideal of unselfish romantic love, and they use biblical imagery to depict a profound sense of alienation and despair associated with these romantic failures. These include Ernest Hemingway's *The Sun Also Rises* (1926), T. S. Eliot's *The Love Song of J. Alfred Prufrock* (1915), and Eliot's *The Waste Land* (1922).

Of course, the failure of romantic love was represented as devastatingly tragic long before the advent of modernist alienation and despair. Likewise, depictions of friendships, familial relationships, and romantic love as being profoundly meaningful in both their successes and failures did not originate in biblical descriptions of God as a friend, father, and husband. Even so, when writing about the importance of human relationships in cultural contexts that have been strongly influenced by the Bible, authors can inadvertently create a sense of resonance with this biblical theme. When such works explicitly invoke the Bible, the resonance can become symphonic.

Shakespeare's *Othello* (c. 1603), for example, might be said to reverse the biblical imagery by which adultery can serve as a metaphor for turning away from God. The play suggests that literal (non-metaphorical) adultery is not about sex—at least not primarily; instead, sexual betrayal becomes a metaphor for being unfaithful. By focusing on what turns out to be a sexual non-event (the alleged sexual infidelity of Othello's wife, Desdemona), the play implies that a lack of trust is the fundamental problem. Moreover, that problem is primarily Othello's, not Desdemona's. He turns out to be the adulterer, in a sense, and the sin of his unfaithfulness to Desdemona—his lack of trust—gets dramatized in his eventual murder of her.

This biblical interpretation of the play derives from Shakespeare's characterizations of Othello's so-called friend, Iago, who sets out to destroy Othello's trust in Desdemona. Shakespeare casts Iago as a Satanic figure in biblical terms that would have been recognized by most of the play's original audience: "I am not what I am," Iago reveals, which is the negation of the name God gives himself when speaking to Moses (discussed in Chapter 1). When Othello finally realizes that Iago has misled him, Othello's reaction reinforces the earlier biblical allusion: "I look down towards his feet; but that's a fable." As Hannibal Hamlin points out, "Othello half-expects to see the cloven hooves commonly associated with the Devil" (59).

Nathaniel Hawthorne's "Young Goodman Brown" (1835) tells a similar story, only this time the devil is played by the devil himself, and his erosion of Brown's ability to trust ends up poisoning all of Brown's relationships—with friends and family as well as his wife. The devil simply introduces the suspicion that those Brown has trusted might not actually be trustworthy. This suspicion ends up hurting Brown rather than protecting him from the possible unfaithfulness of others—much as the doubt introduced by the serpent in the Garden of Eden ends up hurting Eve. Writing in the same era as Hawthorne, English poet Felicia Hemans declared, "who never was deceived, I would not trust," by which she means that to protect yourself from all possible deception would cause you to assume the worst of other people—which, in turn, would effectively destroy intimacy.

At the same time, writers such as Irish poet Seamus Heaney and American poet and novelist Monique Truong attest that to trust others enough to achieve *agape* is no easy feat. Indeed, doing so arguably requires a leap of faith. The title of Heaney's poem, "Miracle" (2010), might seem to refer to Jesus's miraculous healing of a paralyzed man in Mark 2:1–12. After all, the poem retells that story right down to the men who lowered their paralyzed friend down through a hole in the roof because it was the only way to get their friend close to Jesus. Yet the poem does more than retell that part of the story. It focuses on that part, drawing our attention away from what we might think of as the miracle: "Not the one who takes up his bed and walks / But the ones who have known him all along / And carry him in." They are miraculous, too, the poem contends—or not them, exactly, but what goes on between them, in their relationships with each other, which leads them to work so hard for their friend's sake.

It might be something like a miracle that we human beings trust each other enough to form friendships at all. It is at least thoroughly improbable, according to the narrator and protagonist of Monique

Truong's *The Book of Salt* (2003). Yet is also indispensable, worth hoping for and trying to achieve against all odds and despite all past betrayals. The alternative, according to Truong's novel, is suicide. *The Book of Salt* renders the possibility of trust and human connection more remote and more imperiled by making its protagonist an impoverished queer Vietnamese cook living in 1920s and '30s Paris—a distrusted outsider by virtue of his race, nationality, sexuality, and class, let alone his difficulty speaking French or English. Even while his chances of achieving intimate human relationships are remote, the protagonist refuses to stop loving others, calling out for connection even with those who have rejected him. Arguably most remarkable, the novel uses biblical imagery to symbolize this insistence on human connection, especially drawing on Paul's image of a community composed of very different members who are nonetheless united as one, like the different parts of the human body (noted above).

Many authors—including a significant number who do not consider themselves adherents to any particular religious tradition and who do not necessarily believe in God—have found inspiration in the wealth of biblical imagery that casts intimate human relationships as reflections and even extensions of human relationships with God. Whether used purely metaphorically or as signs of something more, such imagery can help articulate a sense of the profound importance and meaning of human relationships.

SUMMARY

- Personal relationships constitute one of the clearest sets of metaphors the Bible uses to describe God—as a friend, father, lover, or husband.
- In seeking to gain a better understanding of how this set of metaphors works, it is important to survey some of the many rich biblical stories about these types of relationships. Trust and unselfish love are common themes in such stories.
- In biblical stories about family relationships, tensions arise when a parent favors one child over another. Usually such favoritism has destructive consequences.

- The Bible's depictions of God as a lover or husband strike a range of chords, from the viscerally negative to the voluptuously and even transcendently positive.
- The literary legacy of this set of imagery attests to the difficulty of trusting others enough to form intimate relationships but also to how important and meaningful such relationships can be.

QUESTIONS FOR DISCUSSION

1   How literally or metaphorically do you think we should interpret biblical descriptions of God as a friend, father, or husband? For example, is God's "jealousy" purely a metaphor meant to emphasize that the Israelites should not worship other gods? Or is it more literal, implying that turning away from God is like betraying the trust and love of another person? Are there other ways to interpret this metaphor?

2   Is it okay for a parent to have a favorite child? Do biblical depictions of such favoritism represent a possibly deplorable but nonetheless realistic aspect of human experience? If God chooses some people over others, does that raise concerns similar to those raised by biblical depictions of parents playing favorites with their children?

3   During some historical periods more than others, religious believers have felt uncomfortable with the erotic aspect of biblical descriptions of God as a lover and husband. What are your thoughts and feelings about the erotic aspect of this metaphor?

4   This chapter noted two ancient Hebrew and Greek terms that are usually translated as *love* in modern English: *chesed* and *agape*. How would you define the various kinds of love depicted in the Bible? Do these accord with your own definition of *love*? Are there biblical depictions of family, friendship, marriage, or romance that seem to have nothing to do with love?

5   Are you especially fond of a particular portrayal of family, friendships, or romance in a work of literature? Does this portrayal resonate in any way with biblical depictions of such relationships?

SUGGESTIONS FOR FURTHER READING

Consider reading one or more of the literary and biblical texts mentioned above. For additional literary works, try Katherine Anne Porter's "The Jilting of Granny Weatherall" (1930), Bernard Malamud's "Idiots First" (1963), Philip Roth's *Portnoy's Complaint* (1969), Amy Tan's *The Hundred Secret Senses* (1995), or Louise Erdrich's "Satan: Highjacker of a Planet" (1997).

For relevant scholarly work, consider the following:

Alter, Robert. *The Art of Biblical Narrative*. New York: Basic Books, 2011 (rev. edn.). In this now-classic study, Alter illuminates the structure and power of biblical storytelling.

Jack, Alison. *SCM Core Text: The Bible and Literature*. London: SCM Press, 2012. Focusing especially on various methodological practices one might use to study the relationship between the Bible and literature, Jack offers readings of literary text such as "Young Goodman Brown."

Jones, Norman W. "Eucharistically Queer? The Postsecular as Transnational Reading Strategy in *The Book of Salt*." *Studies in American Fiction* 41.1 (2014): 103–29. This essay interprets Monique Truong's novel as a case-study that helps explain the importance of appreciating biblical and more broadly religious themes and allusions in contemporary literature.

Smith, Warren S. "The Wife of Bath Debates Jerome." *The Chaucer Review* 32.2 (1997): 129–45. Smith provides a sense of the historical context for the biblical and theological issues raised by the Wife of Bath story.

3

CRIME AND PUNISHMENT

Given the previous chapter's exploration of the literal and meta-phorical importance of close personal relationships, it should come as no surprise that the most common moral failings in the Bible involve people betraying such relationships. This chapter focuses on biblical depictions of what happens when things go wrong—how betrayals of God and humans get punished, and more broadly what biblical texts tell us about the justice of God. In order to explain the literary legacy of these themes, the chapter first explores them through a reading that treats the Bible as a unified whole. That story, in turn, helps illuminate the tensions within and among biblical texts that lead many to question whether the Bible offers a coherent sense of justice and whether biblical texts depict a God who deserves to be called "just" or "good."

If we view God as the main character of one overarching story, then it seems that one of his primary goals is to create a harmonious world in which people love and trust him, therefore also loving and trusting each other (discussed in Chapter 2; see Leviticus 19:9–18, Deuteronomy 6:5, and Matthew 22:34–40). In storytelling terms, it naturally follows that this protagonist's primary conflict stems from people thwarting that goal. The people God singles out for special trust and blessing—the chosen ones—fail or even betray him. Right from the beginning, Adam and Eve trust the serpent and distrust God (Genesis 3). Abraham, in order to gain favor with Pharaoh, pretends that his wife is his sister and gives her to Pharaoh as a new wife (interestingly, God punishes Pharaoh, not Abraham, for this in Genesis 12). Moses doubts God while leading the Israelites in the desert (Numbers 20). David wantonly breaks God's commandments to satisfy his desire for Bathsheba (2 Samuel 11). Israel as a nation repeatedly turns away from God to worship idols (e.g., Exodus 32, 2 Kings 17, and Jeremiah 2). Peter, one of Jesus' most highly favored disciples, flees when Jesus is taken away to be crucified and denies knowing Jesus three times that night (Matthew 26). And Judas, Jesus' friend and disciple, betrays Jesus with a kiss, identifying him to the authorities so they can execute him (Luke 22:47–8). With friends like these, who needs enemies? In storytelling terms, the people God loves are also his antagonists.

Indeed, if the Bible tells a tale that remains incomplete and even to some extent untellable (as Chapter 1 argues), part of the reason for this seems to be that key biblical texts (such as Revelation) insist that the overarching tale will have a happy ending despite the fact that the protagonist seems unlikely to be able to achieve his goal. After all, if biblical stories are any indication, human beings are unlikely to become truly faithful and loving. It would take a miracle! In the Bible, miraculous intervention remains a possibility, but even that raises difficult questions—questions biblical texts often wrestle with and that have been vigorously debated throughout the Bible's reception history. For starters, if God wants people to love and trust him in an unselfish way, embracing *agape* (as explained in Chapter 2), then is it possible for that goal to be achieved through a crime-and-punishment system of justice, even if the punishments are supernaturally bad and the rewards supernaturally good? Could that goal genuinely be achieved even by God's miraculous over-coming or transformation of the human will to make people love him? Put differently, is a fearful "love" that exists only because it is compelled by threats (if we can call such a thing love)—or a robotic "love" that exists only because it is compelled by a miracle—really the kind of love this protagonist seems to desire?

Many Bible stories suggest not. Instead of compelling people out-right, God woos, threatens, and even sometimes punishes people but also repeatedly gives them the choice to turn away from him—from the Garden of Eden story to the crucifixion of Jesus. Even when God goes to miraculous lengths to compel people, such as by sending a storm and then a giant fish after Jonah, Jonah remains unloving and disgruntled. God commands Jonah to warn the city of Nineveh to change its evil ways to avoid being punished. Yet Jonah flees in the opposite direction because he hates the Ninevites: they are enemies of Israel. God sends a giant fish to bring him back, so Jonah finally fulfills God's command. Yet the success of this warning still leaves Jonah bitter and angry at God (see inset).

As often as biblical stories emphasize morality—differentiating between right and wrong behaviors—they also emphasize that all human beings fail to meet God's moral standards. At the same time, they repeatedly portray God as loving human beings so much ("abounding in steadfast love") that he is willing to forgive them and try to woo them back to repentance, as he does once again with Jonah at the end of that story. In the New Testament he tries to woo people by sending his only son, but he still gives people the choice to reject and even kill Jesus.

One of the most remarkable aspects of the Bible is how deeply flawed its human characters are. It tells tales of deception, betrayal, incest, adultery, rape, and murder that could rival twenty-first-century tabloids and soap operas. Every time I read these stories, I always find myself impressed that the Israelites come off so badly in their own sacred history. I cannot help but admire their

> When God saw what they did, how they turned from their evil ways, God changed his mind about the calamity that he had said he would bring upon them; and he did not do it. But this was very displeasing to Jonah, and he became angry. He prayed to the LORD and said, "O LORD! Is not this what I said while I was still in my own country? That is why I fled to Tarshish at the beginning; for I knew that you are a gracious God and merciful, slow to anger, and abounding in steadfast love, and ready to relent from punishing." (Jonah 3–4)

humility and honesty. Many of the disciples and early followers of Jesus also come off remarkably badly in the stories and letters that came to be revered by Christians as part of their sacred history. Impressively enough, generations of Jews and Christians chose not to edit out their ancestors' failures.

The Mosaic covenant might be said to anticipate these failures in that it includes guidelines for the annual Day of Atonement when all of the Israelites make amends for their sins, their failures to keep God's commandments (Leviticus 16). All Israelites need to atone each year presumably because "there is no one who does not sin," as Solomon declares much later during the dedication of the first temple (1 Kings 8:46). Likewise in the New Testament story of the woman caught in adultery, Jesus issues an ironic command to the men who want to stone her to death: "Let anyone among you who is without sin be the first to throw a stone at her" (John 8:7). After that, none of the men can throw a stone. This story does not appear in some of the earliest manuscripts and therefore may be a later addition, but it has nevertheless played an important role in the Bible's reception history and accords with the general biblical insistence that all people fall short of God's ideal.

This aspect of the Bible seems to be one of many reasons why it has inspired even authors who are not religious: it is not a collection of stories about inhumanly perfect superheroes. Jesus comes closest to fitting that description, and certainly traditional Christian theology considers him to be without sin (a Catholic teaching also considers Mary, his mother, to be without sin). Yet even Jesus struggles with his mission, regularly getting frustrated with people and finally asking God to allow him not to be crucified (Matthew 26:39). In Hebrew scripture, God, too, repeatedly gets frustrated and angry. Many Bible stories seem especially relatable because of their characters' flaws or struggles—including God's struggles. If viewed as the protagonist of a unified narrative, he is at least somewhat relatable insofar as he plays the passionate and frustrated suitor of a feckless and faithless lover.

Even so, this love story raises difficult questions because the protagonist is God, whom the Bible generally represents as the all-powerful and morally good creator of the world. Does God compromise justice by wooing such reprobate lovers, and especially by choosing to favor some reprobates over others? These questions lead to a more fundamental one: is God's world truly just at all? If God is all-powerful, then why did he create a world in which injustice often thrives and the good suffer? Why do some biblical stories depict God as doing or commanding things that seem unjust? And why do different biblical texts imply different notions of justice and morality? This chapter explores the literary legacy of these questions.

GOD'S LAW: ETHICS AND HOLINESS

The Torah or Pentateuch—the first five books of the Bible—are often referred to as "the Law" for a good reason: much of these five books (originally scrolls) describes the extensive laws and instructions given by God to Moses at Mount Sinai. Beginning about halfway through the second book (Exodus), the laws continue through the third book (Leviticus), get intermixed with narrative in the fourth book (Numbers), and finally get retold in Deuteronomy (which literally means "second law").

Christians have generally not held themselves accountable to all of the laws given to Moses, in accordance with Paul's New Testament letter to the Galatians: he argues that the Mosaic law was a temporary measure obviated by the new covenant in Christ. According to Paul, the new covenant fulfills the Mosaic law because it fulfills the older Abrahamic covenant, and the Mosaic covenant was just an extension of the original one with Abraham. Paul even goes so far as to argue against circumcision, the sign of loyalty to this older covenant, by arguing that God chose Abraham even before he instituted circumcision as the sign of the covenant (Romans 4). If God's choice constitutes the original covenant, then the rules that followed are merely secondary. All this points to a contentious question among the early followers of Jesus: do non-Jewish (Gentile) followers of Jesus need to observe the Mosaic law? Shockingly, Paul, a devout Jew who scrupulously observed the law, became the staunchest opponent of such observance for Gentile Christians. He thereby helped inaugurate the creation of Christianity as a religion separate from Judaism.

To understand Galatians and many other biblical texts, you need a basic understanding of Mosaic laws. Scholars categorize these laws in a variety of ways, but for the purposes of this book, a relatively simple two-part distinction will suffice: some laws concern ethics and justice, while others concern holiness and purity. These two types are not listed separately but are often intermingled with each other. The Ten Commandments, for example, divide roughly in half between the two. The first half requires the Israelites to mark their holiness (or more precisely God's holiness) by not worshiping other gods or images (idols), not using God's name lightly, and by resting on the seventh day (the Sabbath). The second half requires the Israelites to treat other people well by respecting their parents and not murdering, stealing, lying, coveting others' possessions, or committing adultery. As discussed in Chapter 2, this two-part structure resonates with the Bible's frequent suggestion that loving people and loving God are intimately interrelated.

The Ten Commandments are just the beginning of the laws (or instructions). The two types of law—ethics and holiness—continue to be intermingled. Many of the ethical injunctions are if-then instructions that constitute a kind of "case law." Deuteronomy 22, for example, offers instructions about what to do if your neighbor's ox or sheep stray onto your land, or if a man wrongly accuses his wife of not having been a virgin before they were married. These laws strive for fairness in ways that generally make sense to modern sensibilities. The holiness instructions, by contrast, can seem mysterious and even arbitrary to modern readers, such as the prohibitions against eating shellfish or pork—or, in Deuteronomy 22:11, against wearing "clothes made of wool and linen woven together."

Scholars have proposed a variety of different rationales for such laws. Twentieth-century anthropologist Mary Douglas created one of the most widely accepted theories. According to Douglas, the holiness laws assume a worldview in which all good things (including clothing, animals, and even people) belong to specific categories—categories not entirely unlike modern scientific categories that classify living things into groups according to similarities and differences. Things that blur or confuse the boundaries between different categories are considered impure or unclean and therefore unholy. So pork is forbidden because pigs have cloven hooves like cows but do not "chew the cud" or ruminate as cows do; cows set the standard for that category, so pigs are impure (Leviticus 11:1–8). Likewise, fish set the standard for aquatic creatures, and they have fins and scales; so shellfish are impure because they are aquatic creatures who have neither fins nor scales (Leviticus 11:9–12). Similarly, animals or humans who are ill or infirm are considered less perfect examples of their categories than those who are "without blemish" (Leviticus 1:3). This kind of value judgment can seem unfair to modern readers because it is based on circumstances beyond an individual's control. As we will see shortly, some parts of the Bible seem to share this concern.

THE JUSTICE OF GOD: PREDICTABLE, MYSTERIOUS, AND APOCALYPTIC

As soon as the law is given to Moses, a series of crime-and-punishment stories reinforce the impression that God swiftly rewards the just and punishes the wicked—an impression already established by earlier biblical stories such as God's destruction of Sodom and Gomorrah by raining fire and brimstone (Genesis 19), and his drowning all the people of the earth except Noah and his family (Genesis 6–9). As Moses leads the Israelites through the desert after receiving the law on Mount Sinai (Mount Horeb in Deuteronomy, which may have been a different name for the same mountain), the Israelites repeatedly disobey or distrust God. God provides water from the rocks and manna to eat, a miraculous bread that rains down from heaven (Exodus 16). Yet the Israelites complain about this food. So God sends quails for them to eat but also a plague that kills many of them (Numbers 11). When they see the land of Canaan where God wants them to live, many Israelites distrust God, fearing that the inhabitants of Canaan will destroy them. So God makes them spend another forty years wandering in the desert (Numbers 13–14). They later complain again, so God sends venomous snakes to bite them. He instructs Moses to make a bronze serpent set high on a pole so that if the Israelites look at it (presumably in repentance), the venom will not kill them (Numbers 21).

This crime-and-punishment theme (with some options for repentance) continues throughout the story of the Israelites' rise and fall as a nation. They conquer the peoples who had been living in Canaan and establish a kingdom in the promised land, but they then become divided, turn away from God, and eventually get conquered by Assyria and Babylon. This story, told in Deuteronomy, Joshua, Judges, and the books of Samuel and Kings, is often called the Deuteronomistic history. It repeatedly insists that God rewards the Israelites' obedience to the Mosaic laws and punishes their disobedience.

Such a predictable and immediate system of rewards and punishments might seem to make a lot of sense, but other biblical texts suggest that God's justice is more mysterious. Psalm 73, for example, attests to "the prosperity of the wicked": the corrupt and haughty are often rich and healthy, and the ungodly are "always at ease; they increase in riches." The Psalm looks forward to a future time when God will punish the wicked, but in the present, evildoers seem to be rewarded. Ecclesiastes more vehemently attests that there is no justice in life: "the race is not to the swift, nor the battle to the strong, nor bread to the wise, nor riches to the intelligent, nor favor to the skillful; but time and chance happen to them all" (Ecclesiastes 9). The same passage also rejects the idea that God will reward good people in an afterlife: "the dead know nothing; they have no more reward, and even the memory of them is lost." (The hopelessness expressed in Ecclesiastes is unusual in the Bible and has traditionally been interpreted as articulating the kind of rock-bottom despair that sometimes leads a person to turn to God.)

In the New Testament, Jesus explains his injunction to "love your enemies and pray for those who persecute you" by pointing out that God exemplifies this ideal: God "makes his sun rise on the evil and on the good, and sends rain on the righteous and on the unrighteous" (Matthew 5). Certain Gospel stories also undermine the belief (which seems to have been fairly widespread in the ancient Near East) that illness and infirmities are caused by misdeeds. When Jesus heals the paralyzed man (discussed in Chapter 2), he distinguishes between forgiving the man's sins and healing his paralysis (Mark 2). Elsewhere, Jesus rejects the suggestion that a man's blindness was caused by sin (John 9). Sometimes, the New Testament does imply a predictable and immediate system of rewards and punishments, such as in one of the stories about the early Christian community. Ananias and Sapphira agree to share their wealth equally with the community but then renege and lie about it, so God strikes them dead (Acts 5). Likewise, when the apostles get thrown in jail for preaching about Jesus, God frees them (Acts 5, 12, 16). Yet even in the Book of Acts, not all stories imply this system of justice: Stephen gets stoned to death for preaching about Jesus, and God grants him a vision but does not rescue him (Acts 7).

Hebrew scripture articulates these tensions most famously in the Book of Job, which implicitly questions not only whether a

Theodicy refers to attempts to explain the justice of God, especially why a good and all-powerful God would allow evil to exist. Put simply, why do bad things happen to good people?

predictable and immediate system of rewards and punishments exists but also whether such a system would be adequate to God's purposes. Job is a good man who is faithful to God but nevertheless suffers terrible calamities, losing all his children and his wealth. He also loses his health: his body is covered in sores. His friends interpret these ills as God's punishment for wrongdoings; they urge Job to repent so that his fortunes might be restored. Job objects, insisting that he has done nothing wrong. His friends see this as yet another sin: everyone sins, after all, so everyone deserves to be punished. Even if Job did nothing terribly sinful himself, surely one of his family members sinned? They try to convince Job that he should be grateful for his calamities because this is how God corrects and instructs people (Job 5). All of these explanations accord with certain other biblical texts, and all of them have played prominent roles in the Bible's reception history. Yet Job rejects them all.

In the end, God speaks to Job out of a whirlwind (as discussed in Chapter 1). God's answer to Job's questions is really a non-answer because he responds only with his own question: how can a human being possibly understand God? Surprisingly enough, however, God condones Job for his faith and reproves Job's friends: he commands them to repent for the way they counseled Job. The story has traditionally been interpreted as suggesting that God's justice is a mystery, something human beings can trust but cannot fully understand. In this light, Job's friends get rebuked for their certainty, their unwarranted confidence that they understand God.

In a characteristically biblical dramatic irony, the reader knows from the beginning of the story that Job's friends are wrong. Job suffers not for any sins but because of an argument between God and Satan, an adversarial figure in the heavenly court whose name literally suggests something like a prosecuting attorney. Satan claims that Job's faithful goodness results merely from his prosperity. Take away his good fortune, Satan says, "and he will curse you to your

From the Greek word for revelation or unveiling, **apocalyptic** writings use symbolic visions to reassure readers that in the future God will reward the faithful and punish the wicked. Historically, apocalyptic writings have reassured those who saw themselves as persecuted and oppressed. Today, *apocalyptic* is often used to describe disastrous cataclysms. This is because apocalyptic writings in the Bible describe the world ending in such cataclysms (wars, natural disasters, and supernatural scourges) before God creates an eternally peaceful and just kingdom on earth.

face" (Job 1:11). God disagrees but allows Satan to test the theory. (Many people read Job not as a history book but as an extended parable; it is worth considering how each of these two different ways of viewing the book might change your interpretation of it, especially God's seeming cruelty in allowing Satan to torture Job and kill his children).

Readers often overlook a remarkable aspect of this arrangement between God and Satan: God seems to agree with Satan's assumption that Job's faithful goodness is not so impressive or significant if it derives merely from a system of predictable and immediate rewards and punishments. This assumption resonates with the theme of friendship explored in Chapter 2: many biblical texts champion the kind of love described by Paul as *agape*, a form of love not motivated by the desire for personal gain. So what motivates this unselfish form of love? What motivates Job's loyalty to God even when he has nothing left to lose (Job 7)? We are not told. It is important enough to set the story in motion, but the story does not directly explain it.

Christian interpreters traditionally read Job as pointing to a third biblical notion of God's justice, namely the hope for an afterlife—an everlasting life in which God's justice will finally become clear. This hope is typically intertwined with an expectation that human history as we know it will eventually come to an end, the *eschaton*, which will entail God's final judgment and renewal of the world. Somehow, in the end, all wrongs will be righted.

When you hear of wars and rumors of wars, do not be alarmed; this must take place, but the end is still to come. For nation will rise against nation, and kingdom against kingdom; there will be earthquakes in various places; there will be famines. This is but the beginning of the birth pangs. ... Then they will see "the Son of Man coming in clouds" with great power and glory. Then he will send out the angels, and gather his elect from the four winds, from the ends of the earth to the ends of heaven. (Mark 13)

The New Testament strongly anticipates the end of history, but the expectation also appears in the Old Testament book of Daniel: its seventh chapter exemplifies what has come to be called *apocalyptic writing* (see inset on p.95). Four strange and violent beasts wreak havoc for a time before the Son of Man, "coming with the clouds of heaven," is given an "everlasting" kingdom on earth by God, "the Ancient of Days." Many scholars think the Book of Daniel was composed centuries after the Babylonian captivity and that it recalls that earlier period of foreign oppression to help inspire its readers to remain faithful to God under the threat of some later foe (perhaps Greek forces). Shadrach, Meshach, and Abednego remain faithful to God despite the threat of death. Even when they get thrown into a fiery furnace as a result, God protects them such that they emerge unscathed (Daniel 3). Daniel likewise gets locked into a den of hungry lions for refusing to abandon his faith, and God protects him (Daniel 6). The apocalyptic vision in Daniel 7 may thus be seen as continuing this theme of steadfast faith, reassuring readers that no matter how bad things look now, they can still trust that God will eventually make all things right: "Many of those who sleep in the dust of the earth shall awake, some to everlasting life, and some to shame and everlasting contempt" (Daniel 12:2). (Notably, this is one of very few passages in Hebrew scripture that suggests rewards and punishments in an afterlife.)

In the New Testament, Matthew, Mark, and Luke allude to Daniel's apocalyptic vision, referring to Jesus as "the Son of Man" who will return at some unknown time in the future to usher in God's kingdom on earth. Judging by the letters of Paul, early Christians expected that Jesus might return at any moment.

This expectation also informs the final book of the Bible, Revelation, which uses imagery similar to that found in Daniel 7 to describe its apocalyptic vision of the *eschaton* or end-times. Seven seals are broken, seven trumpets sound, and seven bowls of wrath are poured out; these bring various calamities on earth, including four horsemen unleashed in the process. The "kings of the whole world" gather for battle at Armageddon, a name that may refer to the region of Meggido where many ancient battles were fought (Revelation 16:14–16). An evil woman rides upon a seven-headed beast; her forehead bears the inscription, "Babylon the great, mother of whores" (Revelation 17–18). Babylon (the ancient enemy of Israel and Judah) most likely represents Rome (the late first-century CE enemy of Christians). Another beast bears a "mark" that is "the name of the beast or the number of its name," 666 (or 616 in some manuscripts), which appears to be code for the Emperor Nero (Revelation 13). Both Nero and Domitian, another Roman emperor, persecuted Christians. Revelation was probably written toward the end of the first century CE during Domitian's reign.

The primary message of Revelation seems to accord with apocalyptic writings in general: despite how bad things seem at present, God remains in charge. He is "the Alpha and the Omega"—literally the first and last letters of the Greek alphabet but figuratively the beginning and end of all things (Revelation 1:8 and 22:13). He will punish the wicked and reward the faithful when Christ returns to establish God's kingdom on earth (Revelation 19–22).

FREE WILL AS AN EXPLANATION FOR INJUSTICE

The above discussion illustrates three ways in which the Bible depicts God's justice, but why does an all-powerful God allow injustice in the first place? The traditional Augustinian theodicy (explanation of God's justice) holds that injustice exists because of free will. God allows people to choose evil because this free will enables the existence of a greater good—namely, the potential for moral goodness, for choosing right over wrong. Presumably God could create a world of robotic automatons, but this would preclude true moral goodness because it would preclude moral choices. The value of moral goodness outweighs the evils enabled by free will. This Augustinian theodicy resonates with the Book of Job's suggestion that true goodness and faith should be motivated by something more profound than a simple system of rewards and punishments. Job and other biblical stories imply that this "something more," this costly greater good, does not seem to be easily articulated or comprehended. The disciples, for example, cannot understand what greater good would lead Jesus to allow himself to be crucified.

Throughout the Bible's reception history, believers seeking to understand biblical depictions of God's justice have developed a complex theological and philosophical tradition of thinking about the concept of free will. Does "free" will exist? If free will explains why God allows evil to exist, can the benefits of such freedom outweigh the horrific suffering so often evident in the world—including not only such man-made evils as the Holocaust but also the suffering caused by disease and natural disasters? The complex tradition of wrestling with these questions lies beyond the scope of this book, but the complexity itself attests to the ongoing difficulty of articulating the mysterious "something more" at issue in many biblical depictions of moral choices (e.g. Matthew 5:46–8).

Some contend that the Bible's use of stories to help articulate the justice of God—perhaps most visibly in the parables of Jesus but also in the larger Gospel narratives, in the predominance of narrative in Hebrew scripture, and in that the Mosaic law itself is set within a frame narrative—seems appropriate to the concept of free will because stories tend to encourage people to interpret and judge for themselves. By comparison with expository arguments, stories typically present more ambiguities and interpretive possibilities. For starters, we can usually identify with various different characters' perspectives, let alone that stories often invite figurative interpretations. Stories can thus seem to fit well with Jesus' exhortation to "judge for yourselves" (Luke 12:57).

According to those who view this exhortation as a key to how to read the Bible, many biblical stories are not meant to be simple or clear but are meant to be wrestled with. Such stories can thereby challenge readers to come to their own conclusions much as Nathan's story leads David to judge his own actions (as discussed in the introduction). Such was the argument made by nineteenth-century

Danish philosopher Søren Kierkegaard, who famously wrestled with one of the most morally challenging episodes in the Bible: the story of how God asks Abraham to kill his son, Isaac, as a holy sacrifice (Genesis 22). It came to be known as "the Akedah," the binding, which refers to Abraham's tying Isaac before laying the boy on top of an altar and raising the knife to kill him. For Kierkegaard, the ethical violation at the heart of this story cannot be resolved; the story thus illustrates a paradoxical sense of faith beyond reason. How can it be just for God to ask Abraham to sacrifice a human being, let alone a child, let alone his own son? Isaac was the miracle child of Abraham and Sarah's old age (Genesis 21). How could Abraham obey this command to kill the boy and burn his body as a sacrifice to God? At the last minute, an angel cries out and stops him: it was a test of Abraham's loyalty to God, who miraculously provides a ram to be sacrificed in place of Isaac. Is this an unnecessarily cruel test of faith, perhaps not unlike God's allowing Satan to test Job?

Some read the Akedah as similar to the Book of Job in that both arguably invite readers to trust not a clearly explained system of justice but rather a promise made by God. They invite us to trust not a system but a person, figuratively speaking. God's response to Job does not clearly answer Job's questions, but God's presence seems sufficient for Job. Similarly, when Isaac asks his father why they brought no lamb for the offering they are preparing, Abraham's answer might suggest that he trusts God not to make him sacrifice the boy: "God himself will provide the lamb for a burnt offering" (Genesis 22:7–8). For some, these stories suggest a cruel and despotic God; for others, however, they resonate with apocalyptic writings, asking readers to trust that somehow, in the end, all will be well.

Christian traditions often suggest that God's justice finds its fullest expression in the notion of grace, a simultaneous insistence on both justice and mercy that points beyond ordinary human understandings of justice, beyond the logic of crime and punishment, to "something more"—to a kind of love not fully or clearly comprehensible in ordinary human terms. In these traditions, the notion of grace constitutes a point of convergence among biblical depictions of God as both transcendent and immanent. The story of God's love may be a tale that cannot be fully or clearly told, but the story can be told at least fully and clearly enough to allow for the moral choice to trust God's promise.

> The days are surely coming, says the LORD, when I will make a new covenant with the house of Israel and the house of Judah. It will not be like the covenant that I made with their ancestors when I took them by the hand to bring them out of the land of Egypt—a covenant that they broke, though I was their husband, says the LORD. But this is the covenant that I will make with the house of Israel after those days, says the LORD: I will put my law within them, and I will write it on their hearts; and I will be their God, and they shall be my people. No longer shall they teach one another, or say to each other, "Know the LORD," for they shall all know me, from the least of them to the greatest, says the LORD; for I will forgive their iniquity, and remember their sin no more. (Jeremiah 31:31–4)

A nineteenth-century German philosopher, Ludwig Feuerbach, argued for a secular interpretation of God's justice. God is merely a fictional projection of human ideals, according to Feuerbach, and the tensions and complexities of biblical depictions of God's justice reflect not puzzle pieces to be arranged into one unified whole but rather records of historical changes in human understandings of morality. The earlier stories represent God as an externalized expression of primitive moral ideals, whereas later biblical stories represent the internalization of more sophisticated ideals. Thus Jesus reinterprets Mosaic laws as applying not only to actions but also thoughts: you need not actually commit adultery in order to sin; a lustful look will suffice (Matthew 5:27–8). Likewise, you need not commit murder to be "liable to judgment"; being angry with your brother will suffice (Matthew 5:21–4). These changes resonate with a passage from the Old Testament prophet Jeremiah where God promises a "new covenant": "I will put my law within them, and I will write it on their hearts" (see inset).

It is worth noting that the Ten Commandments include a primarily internal prohibition against being covetous. Yet in broad terms, consider how Feuerbach's interpretation illuminates similarities and differences between the story of Moses confronting Pharaoh, on the one hand, and Jesus confronting Pilate, on the other. The Gospel of Matthew casts Jesus as a new Moses: saved as a baby from a massacre of innocent children, he leads his people to a new covenant with God and, in the process, gets transfigured with shining light during a mountain-top meeting with God. Pharaoh and Pilate both think they are in control, but both have their commands thwarted by God: God saves the Hebrews from Pharaoh's injustice much as he resurrects Jesus after Pilate has him crucified. Yet Pharaoh's drama differs from Pilate's because God seems to control Pharaoh almost like a puppet, whereas Pilate suffers internal conflict. God repeatedly "hardened Pharaoh's heart" so that he would not let the Hebrews go (Exodus 4:21, 7:13, 9:12, 10:1, 10:20, 11:10, and 14:8). Pilate, by contrast, publicly washes his hands with water to show that he feels forced to condemn Jesus against his own will: "I am innocent of this man's blood" (Matthew 27:24; the other Gospels do not portray him as so conflicted). Pilate's guilty conscience has inspired such literary homages as that in Shakespeare's *Macbeth* (c. 1606) when Lady Macbeth tries to wash imaginary blood from her hands (5.1).

A still more modern and secular interpretation of biblical ethics holds that the various tensions and complexities charted in this chapter are neither puzzle pieces nor artifacts of progressive development but simply a confusion of disconnected fragments. In keeping with the modern view of the Bible outlined in Chapter 1, the various fragments derive from different sources and reflect different cultural viewpoints that often disagree with each other about God's justice.

Many biblical stories can seem morally reprehensible from a modern standpoint. Why does Lot, who seems to be the good guy in the story of Sodom and Gomorrah, offer his virgin daughters to be raped by the men of Sodom (Genesis 19)? Why does God choose to give the Israelites a land already inhabited by other people, and why does he command the Israelites to kill all those people? How can it be just for God to kill all the firstborn Egyptian children, especially when he forces Pharaoh to keep persecuting the Hebrews (Exodus 11)? The plague of death may constitute a form of poetic justice for Pharaoh's earlier mass killing of Hebrew children, but killing more children seems to offer no literal justice. Similarly troubling, Psalm 137 calls for the violent death of Babylonian children in return for the Babylonian destruction of Israel: "Happy shall they be who take your little ones and dash them against the rock!" Continuing this vindictive theme, a group of children make fun of the prophet Elisha because he is bald, so he causes a bear to maul them to death (2 Kings 2:23–4).

Some troubling biblical stories make at least a bit more sense when we take into account how they reflect different sociocultural mores. For example, when reading about Sodom and Gomorrah or the similar story about the Levite and his concubine, it is worth remembering that showing hospitality to strangers was far more important in ancient Near Eastern cultures than in most modern ones (Genesis 19 and Judges 19). The story of Judah and Tamar might sound outrageously scandalous: after Tamar's husband dies, she tricks her father-in-law, Judah, into having sex with her (Genesis 38). Yet she is the hero of the story because Judah had not made his sons fulfill the Levirate marriage custom. According to this custom, if a man's brother is married but dies childless, then the man must have sex with his brother's widow and raise her children as if they are the deceased brother's. That way, the family line will continue. This custom also helps explain the challenge posed to Jesus about the possibility of an afterlife (Matthew 22:23–33). If a woman has been married to multiple brothers in keeping with the Levirate marriage custom, then whose wife will she be in the afterlife?

Other stories reflect tensions that might be more difficult to resolve. Numbers 23:19 insists, for example, that "God is not a human being, that he should lie, or a mortal, that he should change his mind." Yet the story of the golden calf depicts God as changing his mind. While Moses speaks with God on Mount Sinai, the Israelites create a golden statue of a calf to worship as their new god (Exodus 32). Incensed, God decides to destroy the Israelites. Yet Moses objects: he argues that the Egyptians will hear of the destruction and conclude that the Israelites' God is deceitful and malevolent. Apparently persuaded by this reasoning, God "changed his mind" (Exodus 32:14).

Many readers find God's actions arbitrary and cruel. Romans 9:13 contends that even before Jacob and his twin brother, Esau, were born—before either one had done anything good or bad—God "loved Jacob" but "hated Esau." Augustine cited this as evidence that God predestines some people to be chosen and not others, adding that we simply do not know why. The story of Joseph likewise suggests that God is a kind of puppeteer behind all human actions.

His brothers sell him into slavery, but years later when they discover that he eventually prospered and helped Egypt prepare for a famine with God's help, Joseph tries to assuage their guilt: "do not be distressed, or angry with yourselves, because you sold me," he reassures them, because "it was not you who sent me here, but God," to save their family from the famine (Genesis 45). Various theories attempt to answer the questions about free will implicitly raised by these texts. Whatever your take on such questions, the questions have influenced imaginative literature more than any particular answer.

LITERARY LEGACIES I: RADICAL LOVE AND THE ARTISTIC IMAGINATION

A variety of authors have been inspired by the idea of interpreting God's grace as radical in the sense of subverting ordinary human legal systems of crime and punishment. This idea has appealed even to authors who reject traditional religion, such as Percy Shelley. In *A Defence of Poetry* (1821), Shelley quotes the Bible against those who judge right and wrong only in terms of material "utility." He argues that English "promoters of utility" have created extremes of wealth and poverty—"the rich have become richer, and the poor have become poorer"—and he quotes from the Bible to criticize this inequality: "to those who have, more will be given, and they will have an abundance; but from those who have nothing, even what they have will be taken away" (Matthew 13:12; Shelley uses the King James translation, but I use the New Revised Standard Version (NRSV) for the sake of clarity).

The irony here lies in the original biblical source of the quotation as much as in Shelley's use of it. According to human calculations, it would likely seem fairest to distribute material wealth as equally as possible (Jesus' first followers are described as doing exactly that in Acts 4:32–5). In the quotation, however, Jesus is explaining why he uses parables to teach about God, so the quotation implies a figurative level of interpretation on which material possessions ("abundance") represent spiritual wealth. Yet these two levels of meaning also contrast with one another: while other Gospel passages show Jesus advocating for more equitable sharing of material wealth, he suggests in this quotation that God's justice in spiritual matters works quite differently. Shelley's use of the quotation heightens the ironic tension in the original source because Shelley uses it to refer to material wealth. Yet he also thereby invokes Jesus' implicit message about a very different spiritual way of calculating justice, at least for readers who know the Bible. For Shelley, we access this spiritual level of understanding not through divine revelation from God but through the literary imagination (especially through poetry). It is this literary or poetic imagination that he hopes will serve to correct the man-made injustice of tremendous inequality in material wealth.

So while he decries what he sees as the "gross superstitions" associated with traditional Christian religion, Shelley nevertheless affirms the prophetic biblical notion that true justice lies beyond what he calls "the calculating faculty." For Shelley, we come to understand this mysterious sense of justice not through divine revelation but rather through "the imagination." Shelley is confident that the human imagination—especially as expressed in great poetry—can correct the ill effects of the "unmitigated exercise of the calculating faculty," which runs amok when it neglects "those first principles that belong to the imagination." Indeed, he casts this moral corrective as a primary justification for the importance of poetry.

Many scholars see Shelley as having helped to inaugurate what has been called a religious approach or attitude toward imaginative literature. This attitude gave a kind of blessing to or authority for the nineteenth-century rise of the study of modern (not just ancient) literature as part of university curriculums. Recent scholars challenge the longstanding view that literature in this period increasingly came to be seen as a replacement for religion (an idea often associated with nineteenth-century English poet and critic Matthew Arnold). New research shows that literature was more commonly understood as an extension of religious faith even if it sometimes radically refigured that faith. Shelley, for example, helps make imaginative literature seem more religious and more closely allied with the Bible while also making it seem at the same time more secular. He emphasizes the poetic imagination as the key to and source of this alliance. He also dismisses what he considers mere superstition, in effect attempting to remove God from the equation. God thus becomes merely metaphorical for Shelley—a figurative representation of the human imagination. As with the discussion of Shelley in Chapter 1, what is striking about his views on morality and the human imagination is not that he rejects traditional Christian teachings but that he still subscribes to some of them. Even in his rejection of religion, he continues to be inspired by the Bible.

While Shelley was opposed to the religious authorities of his day, his views bear striking similarities with those of certain religious authors of the eighteenth and nineteenth centuries. Russian novelist Fyodor Dostoevsky, for instance, seems to share something like Shelley's disdain for the human "calculating faculty": Dostoevsky implicitly argues against a utilitarian conception of morality in his 1866 *Crime and Punishment* (which inspired the title of this chapter). William Blake, a radical Christian whose work did not become widely esteemed until the late nineteenth century, similarly rejects what he calls "systematic reasoning" in favor of inspiration and creative energy. In *The Marriage of Heaven and Hell* (1790–3) he avers, "Jesus was all virtue and acted from impulse, not from rules." For Blake, divine justice lies beyond human rules. By comparison with the religious authorities of his day, Blake was perhaps as radical in his Christian beliefs as Shelley was in his atheism, but both found similar inspiration for their radical poetry in the Bible.

Blake promotes what he sees as a biblical sense of anti-systematic divine virtue by reinterpreting one of the Bible's most famous rule books, Proverbs. He anticipates the ire of conventional churchgoers who are fond of clear, systematic rules. Such people will see his proverbs as "Proverbs of Hell." For Blake, self-righteous and overly moralistic Christians are complicit in the very crimes they condemn: "Prisons are built with the stone of Law, Brothels with the bricks of Religion." As anti-religious as this might sound, it could be seen as according with certain traditional interpretations of Paul's New Testament writings about the law: "if it had not been for the law, I would not have known sin" (Roman 7:7). So it should not surprise us when one of the Proverbs of Hell seems to be a straightforward echo of Jesus' teaching about the greatest form of love: "The most sublime act is to set another before you." Thus Blake's title, *The Marriage of Heaven and Hell*, refers to the ironic undermining of what Blake considers overly simplistic notions of heaven and hell, right and wrong, which fail to comprehend how the grace of God remains beyond human systems of morality. For Blake, the figurative nature of art and the intuitive creativity of the artistic imagination are especially well suited to representing this notion of God's grace.

One can see the contemporary legacy of these eighteenth- and nineteenth-century uses of biblical themes and imagery in such works as Australian novelist Patrick White's *Riders in the Chariot* (1961) and American novelist Marilynne Robinson's *Gilead* (2004). *Riders in the Chariot* offers a Blakean articulation of the redemptive possibilities in transgression, suffering, and atonement. *Gilead* constitutes an extended literary meditation on the grace required for forgiveness, a grace represented as transcending ordinary human calculations of merit: "Love is holy because it is like grace—the worthiness of its object is never really what matters." Indeed, similar literary articulations of something like this notion of grace abound in contemporary literature. White and Robinson are just two of many authors who explicitly represent such grace in biblical terms.

LITERARY LEGACIES II: MONSTERS

A more ancient aspect of the Bible's influence on literary depictions of morality and justice can be traced back to one of the earliest surviving literary compositions in English, *Beowulf*, which was probably composed between the eighth and eleventh centuries CE. The eponymous hero must fight the monster, Grendel—after which he fights Grendel's mother and later a dragon, too, for good measure. From *Beowful* to J. R. R. Tolkien's *The Lord of the Rings* (1954–5) and beyond, authors have created tales of good and evil in which evil is embodied in the form of such monsters. Literary depictions of battles between good heroes and evil monsters might appear to represent an oversimplified distinction between good and evil, but these monsters are generally more complex than that.

Battles between heroes and monsters might also seem to imply something close to a dualistic sense of the world whereby good and evil are evenly matched. Yet orthodox Christian worldviews are not dualistic: God is always the undisputed victor before any battle ever begins. Even in more or less Christian monster stories, however, the struggle will likely seem boring if the reader can tell from the outset that the heroes will defeat the evil monsters. Despite having to navigate between this Scylla and Charybdis of either falsifying Christian tradition or boring the reader, the most influential of such stories often manage to tease out important complexities and tensions not only in their characters but also in the Bible.

In *Beowulf*, for example, the monster Grendel is cast as evil in Christian terms, an exiled enemy of God: the poem introduces Grendel as one of "that woeful breed" of giants and evil spirits descended from Cain, the first murderer. In other words, the monster, although a monster, is the descendant of humans and as such potentially blurs what might at first seem like clear boundaries between human and monster, good and evil. Indeed, Grendel is introduced not as a vicious creature but a sad one, "wan-mooded," suffering under God's punishment for his ancestor's crime. Further humanizing him, Grendel has a mother who cares for him and who later seeks to avenge her son's death after Beowulf kills Grendel.

The rich complexity of Grendel was well understood by Tolkien, whose 1936 lecture, "*Beowulf*: The Monster and the Critics," gave readers new ways of appreciating the ancient poem. Tolkien's *Lord of the Rings* trilogy similarly features a monstrous character who, as the reader only gradually discovers, was once the same type of creature—a hobbit—as the story's heroes. Gollum was slowly turned into a monster in part by his own choices but also in part by an evil power beyond his control, an insidious power that imposes on his will and eventually corrupts it even as it confers special powers. Tolkien describes this "Ring of Power" as possessing its own will, a will that eventually comes to dominate the will of anyone who uses it for too long. Critics have pointed out that the tantalizing powers conferred by this ring (such as invisibility), which are hard to resist, might aptly be described as *addictive* in terms of their effect on the wearer's will.

Issues of addiction and willpower loom large in many twenty-first-century societies, from drug addiction to the diet industry to psychopharmacology. Advances in neuroscience suggest that many behaviors once considered a simple matter of willpower probably derive instead from a more complex array of influences, some of which have nothing to do with conscious individual choices. Anthropologists, sociologists, and cultural studies scholars have shown myriad ways in which seemingly individual choices are not only given meaning but are also enabled or foreclosed to a significant extent by an individual's socialization into specific cultural contexts. Modernity has also furnished horrifying examples of how individual choices can be swayed by what psychologists call "groupthink," in which the desire to maintain a harmonious identification with a particular group can lead to irrational and dehumanizing attitudes and actions toward people perceived as outsiders.

Thus biblically inflected stories about malevolent forces that impinge on the will and even turn people into monsters can appear quite relevant in twentieth- and twenty-first-century literature. Hebrew scripture includes accounts of malevolent spiritual forces, such as the "evil spirit" that enters King Saul (1 Samuel 16:14). The New Testament describes these evil forces more frequently. Not only does Satan "enter" Judas before he betrays Jesus (John 13:27), but also Jesus heals many who are possessed by demons (e.g., Matthew 8:28–33, Mark 1:32–4, and Luke 4:33–6). In some parables, Jesus describes an "enemy" at work in the world, "the evil one," "Satan" (Matthew 13:1–30 and Mark 4:15).

Interestingly, New Testament demons might be said to believe in Jesus in the sense that they do not hesitate to acknowledge his divinity: "What have you to do with us, Son of God? Have you come here to torment us before the time?" (Matthew 8:29). They believe but oppose him nonetheless—not unlike Satan, who seems to know that Jesus is divine but tries to convince Jesus to abuse his power and worship the devil (Matthew 4:1–11). The story of Satan tempting Jesus in the desert resonates with that of Eve and the serpent in that Eve gets encouraged to eat the forbidden fruit but still gets to choose for herself whether to bite. Both entail disputes about interpretation—how to interpret God's instructions to Adam and Eve or how to interpret holy scripture in the Gospel story—and both frame those interpretive battles as depending on whether Eve and Jesus will choose to distrust, test, or even deny God in order to aggrandize themselves.

John Milton's retelling of the Adam-and-Eve story similarly places the question of such willful self-aggrandizement at the center of its drama. In *Paradise Lost* (1674), Milton strongly emphasizes the role of the tempter, Satan, and in doing so creates a "monster" who is memorable especially because of his all-too-human qualities. The beginning of the story focuses on Satan's choice to rebel against God (an account that derives from debatable interpretations of biblical passages such as Isaiah 14:12–15, Luke 10:18, and Revelation 12:7–9). Defeated and exiled in hell after his attempted rebellion against God, Satan insists that "all is not lost" because he still possesses his "unconquerable will" (1.106). Milton dramatizes Satan's pride in ways that sound less like an inhuman monster than a haughty courtier: when

> If anyone of the house of Israel or of the aliens who reside among them eats any blood, I will set my face against that person who eats blood, and will cut that person off from the people. For the life of the flesh is in the blood; and I have given it to you for making atonement for your lives on the altar; for, as life, it is the blood that makes atonement. (Leviticus 17:10–14)

two angels fail to recognize him, Satan sneers defensively, "Know ye not me? ... / ... Not to know me argues yourselves unknown" (4.828–30). In his opinion, they must truly be nobodies if they do not know the once-illustrious fallen angel by sight.

Some medieval texts suggest that Christians should be ready to engage in a battle of wills with evil spiritual forces. Only in modern times have demons and evil spirits come to seem definitively atavistic and unbelievable to many people. In earlier eras, they played an important role in traditional Christian theodicies: not all evils in the world were attributed to human sins. Today, demons and evil spirits live on for many people only in literature.

Bram Stoker gave new life to these ancient stories through his popular novel, *Dracula* (1897). Stoker depicts vampires in ways designed to bridge what many in the 1890s saw as the growing gap between ancient and modern worldviews, biblical and scientific criteria for truth. Dracula is cast as a demonic being who is the opposite of Christ. He is repelled by crucifixes and converts chosen victims to a kind of life-after-death (although they end up not truly alive but "undead"). He forces these victims to drink his blood as if in a diabolical reenactment of the Catholic Eucharist in which participants consume the body and blood of Jesus that was sacrificed for their forgiveness (discussed in Chapter 4; see Matthew 26:26–8). The vampire's blood-drinking is thus like a religious ritual even while it also, according to the physician, Van Helsing, is compatible with modern science. He theorizes extensively about possible scientific explanations for vampirism.

Dracula's bite enacts a kind of demon possession: it corrupts the victim's will. At first, Dracula gains a measure of suggestive control. Eventually the victims chosen to become vampires turn into monstrous corruptions of their earlier selves. Vampires, after all, cannot be entirely inhuman inasmuch as they look human and were originally fully human. Stoker emphasizes that the will, the capacity for rational self-determination, can be corrupted: one protagonist, Jonathan Harker, nearly loses his sanity because of Dracula; two others, Lucy and Mina, find their minds partially under Dracula's sway, as does Renfield, a patient in a nearby insane asylum.

Stoker's vampire exemplifies biblically-influenced modern monsters who threaten more than bodily harm: they threaten to corrupt the will itself. In many later vampire stories inspired by Stoker's novel, the battle between good and evil entails a contest not only of ingenuity but also willpower. At first, the victim's will is protected: the vampire must be invited. Yet most vampires are depicted as charming and sexually alluring; if the victim gives in to these temptations, then the victim's will quickly becomes compromised. Several theatrical and cinematic vampire stories dramatize this battle of wills explicitly. Perhaps the most iconic example is Tod Browning's 1931 film, *Dracula*, in which the vampire attempts to use his powers of mind control on Van Helsing: the hero nearly loses this face-off but finally musters sufficient willpower to resist.

From *Beowulf* to *Dracula* and beyond, biblically-influenced monster stories tend to raise questions of free will and its corruption by portraying the monster as significantly human to some extent. Such stories thereby suggest the potential for evil in all people, heroes as well as villains. They also often suggest the potential for redemption in even monstrous villains. In many of the most memorable monster-battle stories, these potential inner conflicts create dramatic tensions and plot-twists that turn out to be at least as engaging for readers as the question of who will win.

SUMMARY

- The Mosaic laws can be categorized by distinguishing between those pertaining to ethics versus those pertaining to holiness.
- Some biblical texts cast God as punishing the wicked and rewarding the faithful in this life according to predictable laws. Other texts suggest that God's justice defies

conventional human understandings of justice—or that it will become clear only at the end of history or in an afterlife.

- Certain biblical texts seem to challenge the idea that the Bible articulates one unified moral system.
- The idea of God's grace as transcending utilitarian calculations of right versus wrong has influenced both the writing and study of imaginative literature. It has arguably influenced the modern concept of "literature" itself.
- Monster stories constitute one of the most interesting biblically-influenced literary traditions of representing moral conflict and the limits of free will.

QUESTIONS FOR DISCUSSION

1   Do biblical depictions of God's justice—his laws, punishments, and mercies—seem compelling or troubling to you? Which specific depictions seem most striking, whether positively or negatively?

2   Must you believe in a Jewish, Christian, or Muslim understanding of God in order to find biblical depictions of ethical standards and failings compelling or useful?

3   Does morality seem to you to be a reasonably straightforward matter? Or do distinctions between right and wrong often seem to involve complex "gray" areas?

4   Do you think free will exists? Why, or why not? If not, then to what extent is it fair to hold people individually accountable for their actions?

5   Do you have a favorite literary work that focuses on justice—on crime and punishment? If so, does it allude to or resonate with the Bible?

6   Are you a fan of any monster stories that resonate with the biblical themes discussed in this chapter?

SUGGESTIONS FOR FURTHER READING

Consider reading one or more of the literary and biblical texts mentioned above. Additional literary works worth exploring include

Samuel Taylor Coleridge's *Rime of the Ancient Mariner* (1789), Alan Paton's *Cry, The Beloved Country* (1948), and Archibald MacLeish's *J.B.* (1958). Regarding Coleridge, see Joseph McQueen's "'Old Faith Is Often Modern Heresy': Re-Enchanted Orthodoxy in Coleridge's 'The Eolian Harp' and *The Rime of the Ancient Mariner*" in *Christianity and Literature* 64.1 (2014): 21–42.

Additional nonfiction works worth consulting include the following:

D'Costa, Gavin. "Atonement and the Crime of Seeing: Patrick White's *Riders in the Chariot.*" *Literature & Theology* 22.2 (June 2008): 162–79. D'Costa reads the novel as drawing on multiple spiritual traditions while also affirming a prophetic and even religious role for literature itself. He cites William Blake as a model for White's complex engagement with transgression, suffering, and atonement.

Goldsmith, Steven. *Unbuilding Jerusalem: Apocalypse and Romantic Representation.* Ithaca: Cornell University Press, 1993. Goldsmith explores the influence of apocalyptic writing in Romantic literature. For more on biblical influences in Romanticism, see the reading suggestions at the end of Chapter 1 as well as Leslie Tannenbaum, *Biblical Tradition in Blake's Early Prophecies: The Great Code of Art.* Princeton: Princeton University Press, 1982.

Hallab, Mary Y. *Vampire God: The Allure of the Undead in Western Culture.* Albany, NY: State University of New York Press, 2009. Hallab's third chapter addresses the issue of free will in Stoker's *Dracula* as well as other vampire stories.

Kaufmann, Michael W. "The Religious, the Secular, and Literary Studies: Rethinking the Secularization Narrative in Histories of the Profession." *New Literary History* 38.4 (2007): 607–27. Kaufmann's essay surveys recent scholarship related to the above discussion of Shelley, Blake, and the nineteenth-century relationship between literature and religion.

4

UNEXPECTED HEROES AND MIRACULOUS RECREATIONS

The last chapter surveyed biblical representations of God's justice. It focused on stories about things going wrong—especially about the consequences of transgressing God's laws. This chapter, by contrast, surveys biblical stories about how wrongs get made right, stories about redemption and renewal. These stories typically entail an ironic reversal of expectations: an unlikely character turns out to be the hero, an unconventional kind of heroism saves the day, or suffering and destruction lead to miraculous restoration and recreation.

A statement is **ironic** if its implied meaning is the opposite of its literal meaning—as when King David's wife, Michal, insults him by at first seeming to praise him: "How the king of Israel honored himself today!" (2 Samuel 6). This is sarcasm, a caustic form of irony that typically uses praise as scorn. Oftentimes, the implied meaning is detectable only from a statement's context. A situation is ironic if it presents the opposite of what we might normally expect, such as when the giant warrior, Goliath, is felled by a boy (1 Samuel 17).

These ironic reversals hold the key to an important question about the Bible's literary reception history: how is it possible that this one book has so often been embraced by both traditionalists and radicals?

Given that Christianity has historically been an integral part of most English-speaking societies, it comes as no surprise that the Bible has often been invoked in the name of traditional religious and political authorities. Yet it has also often been invoked in the name of reform and radical dissent. Among those reformers and dissenters who have been inspired by the Bible stand many of the most influential Anglophone authors, such as John Milton, William Blake, Percy Shelley, Harriet Beecher Stowe, Herman Melville, Walt Whitman, Charles Dickens, Virginia Woolf, Ernest Hemingway, William Faulkner, Toni Morrison, and Salman Rushdie, among others.

This chapter explores biblical stories about unexpected heroes and miraculous recreations—stories that have inspired a wide range of literary works. The opening of the Bible tells how God used words to create the world: "God said, 'Let there be light'; and there was light" (Genesis 1:3). Both traditionally minded and non-traditional authors alike have represented literary creativity as an echo of this miraculous creation of the world. After all, some of the most powerful literature uses words to help readers imaginatively recreate the worlds they think they know.

AN IRONIC MESSIAH?

Readers today often miss some of the unexpected reversals in the Bible because we have been taught to expect them. We are blinded by the Bible's pervasive influence: the primary characters seem so familiar that we think we know them better than we do. Even if we know very little about the Bible, we probably know enough to expect that Jesus will end up crucified instead of living out his life on earth as the political leader of God's special nation. We forget that this seemed shocking and even incomprehensible to his original followers. We therefore fail to appreciate that the New Testament letters and stories show those followers working hard to reinterpret Hebrew scripture in order to understand Jesus' crucifixion and resurrection as a fulfillment of scripture

> He had no form or majesty that we should look at him, nothing in his appearance that we should desire him. He was despised and rejected by others; a man of suffering and acquainted with infirmity; and as one from whom others hide their faces he was despised, and we held him of no account. Surely he has borne our infirmities and carried our diseases; yet we accounted him stricken, struck down by God, and afflicted. But he was wounded for our transgressions, crushed for our iniquities; upon him was the punishment that made us whole, and by his bruises we are healed. All we like sheep have gone astray; we have all turned to our own way, and the LORD has laid on him the iniquity of us all. He was oppressed, and he was afflicted, yet he did not open his mouth; like a lamb that is led to the slaughter, and like a sheep that before its shearers is silent, so he did not open his mouth. (Isaiah 53:2–7)

(e.g., Luke 24:44–7). The crucifixion had at first seemed like a radical departure from Hebrew scripture. Indeed, we might describe the New Testament's relationship to the Old Testament as both radical and traditional at the same time.

Instead of scriptural examples of powerful political heroes such as David and Solomon, early Christians turned to examples of more spiritual heroes such as the "man of sorrows" (or "man of suffering") described by the prophet, Isaiah, in order to help make sense of Jesus' crucifixion. An outcast, misunderstood and rejected by his people, this despised figure ironically turns out to be the hero—the one who heals the very people who "despised and rejected" him (see inset). Wounded for their transgressions, this innocent victim described by Isaiah serves as the means of forgiveness and atonement for all the people, healing them and making them "whole." Christians interpreted this passage as applying to Jesus, in effect explaining how a crucified Messiah could be the hero in terms that reinforced rather than controverted Hebrew scripture.

Isaiah was not the only scriptural text to offer such reinforcement in the eyes of early Christians. While the New Testament stories insist that the disciples were at first shocked and confused by Jesus'

> Then Aaron shall lay both his hands on the head of the live goat, and confess over it all the iniquities of the people of Israel, and all their transgressions, all their sins, putting them on the head of the goat, and sending it away into the wilderness by means of someone designated for the task. The goat shall bear on itself all their iniquities to a barren region; and the goat shall be set free in the wilderness. (Leviticus 16:21–2)

crucifixion and resurrection, these stories also insist that the disciples should not have been so surprised. The language of Isaiah resonates, for example, with the scapegoat used in the Day of Atonement ritual (see inset). The priest is instructed to transfer the sins of the people to a live goat who is then sent out into the wilderness to Azazel, a mysterious figure traditionally associated with Satan (Leviticus 16:8–10). Isaiah suggests that a human being may take the place of this scapegoat; early Christians saw this as Jesus and believed that his crucifixion had made a final, once-and-for-all atonement that would not need to be repeated annually.

They also interpreted Jesus in terms of the most central story of Torah, the Exodus from Egypt when God frees the Israelites from their enslavement. Early Christians especially emphasized the tenth and final plague God sends to convince Pharaoh to let his people go. Each Israelite household sacrifices a lamb and uses its blood to mark the doorposts and lintel of the house in which the lamb is eaten: "When I see the blood, I will pass over you, and no plague shall destroy you when I strike the land of Egypt" (Exodus 12). While the firstborn of every Egyptian household dies, the Israelites remain protected from death. The New Testament parallels the Passover miracle with the crucifixion and resurrection of Jesus. The "last supper" (a term that does not appear in the Bible) Jesus shares with his disciples occurs during the annual Passover commemoration (Matthew 26, Mark 14, and Luke 22), during which Jesus offers bread and wine as his body and blood to be consumed by the disciples. He presents himself as a Paschal lamb (the lamb sacrificed at Passover), and his resurrection marks a kind of permanent Passover in that death itself is defeated, the "last enemy to be destroyed"

> While they were eating, Jesus took a loaf of bread, and after blessing it he broke it, gave it to the disciples, and said, "Take, eat; this is my body." Then he took a cup, and after giving thanks he gave it to them, saying, "Drink from it, all of you; for this is my blood of the new covenant, which is poured out for many for the forgiveness of sins." (Matthew 26:26–8)

(1 Corinthians 15:12–58; see also 2 Timothy 1:10). This victory was celebrated in one of the earliest Christian rituals, "the Lord's supper," in which participants used bread and wine to reenact or commemorate Jesus' self-sacrifice (1 Corinthians 11:17–34). Today, Christians refer to this rite as the Eucharist (which means "thanksgiving") or Communion.

The double imagery of Jesus as both scapegoat and Paschal lamb sometimes causes confusion about whether to use the term *Christ figure* or *scapegoat* to describe characters in literature who resonate with or directly allude to these biblical stories. Both terms refer to innocent outcasts made to suffer for other people's failings, but *Christ figure* most accurately describes a character whose self-sacrifice is willingly chosen. Moreover, this self-sacrifice typically benefits others even if they do not at first understand the benefit. Thus Sydney Carton gives his life to save Charles Darnay and help others in Charles Dickens' *A Tale of Two Cities* (1859). J. K. Rowling offers a more recent example in Harry Potter, who sacrifices himself to save others and defeat the evil Voldemort in *Harry Potter and the Deathly Hallows* (2007). By contrast, Benjy in William Faulkner's *The Sound and the Fury* (1929) is a scapegoat but not a Christ figure. His brother, Jason, unfairly blames Benjy for their family's decline, but Benjy's suffering is not something he willingly chooses (nor is it redemptive for Jason or the other family members).

Jesus saves others by allowing himself to be killed, by suffering, which is why the final week of his life is traditionally referred to as "the Passion": *passion* in this case is from a Greek word meaning *to suffer*. When the Romans crucify Jesus, they place an inscription on his cross that reads, "The King of the Jews" (Mark 15). They intend this as sarcasm, a way to mock Jesus. Yet the Gospel stories are designed to ensure that the reader interprets this differently: the inscription is ironic not because it is false but because it is true. In effect, the Romans unknowingly testify to the truth. New Testament writings frequently allude to Hebrew scripture to justify this ironic interpretation of the long-awaited king or Messiah, such as when Acts 4:10–12 quotes from the Psalms: "The stone that the builders rejected has become the chief cornerstone" (Psalm 118:22). The Gospels quote the same Psalm to suggest that God's promise to Abraham can be extended to Gentiles (non-Jews) through Jesus (Matthew 21:33–46). Indeed, the New Testament seems to embrace this kind of ironic reversal as a general principle whereby outsiders become insiders. Instead of restoring Israel to its former glory as a nation, the Messiah inaugurates a radical reordering of socioeconomic hierarchies: "many who are first will be last, and the last will be first" (Mark 10:31). So Jesus associates himself with those whom the religious authorities find not only sinful but also distasteful, such as prostitutes and tax collectors (collaborators with the Roman occupation).

Again, however, the New Testament casts this radical reordering as traditional by grounding it in Hebrew scripture. After all, power reversals and unexpected heroes are the rule rather than the exception in the Old Testament. King David himself, whose political might the Messiah was expected to restore, was chosen by God to supplant the first king of Israel, Saul. This power reversal resonates not only with the David-and-Goliath story but also with the fact that David was chosen over his older brothers: in ancient Near Eastern cultures, the eldest brother held pride of place over his siblings and was expected to inherit his father's estate (1 Samuel 16). Indeed, such role-reversals among siblings occur regularly enough in the Bible to constitute a theme in its own right. Jacob (whose name suggests "the supplanter") is favored over his older brother, Esau (Genesis 25). Rachel is favored over her older sister, Leah (Genesis 29). Joseph, too, is favored over his older brothers (Genesis 37).

Moses himself is an unlikely hero. Condemned to die as an infant, he instead gets adopted into the household of the enemy leader, Pharaoh. Once grown, Moses at first opposes the injustices perpetrated against his people (the Hebrews or Israelites) but immediately flees to the desert when he realizes that his own life might be at stake in this struggle against oppression (Exodus 2). God finds him in the desert and calls him back to lead the Hebrews to freedom. Yet

Moses objects, arguing that he lacks the skills to be a good leader. Eventually, however, Moses becomes a leader more powerful than Pharaoh.

The story is not unlike that of Gideon. When an angel finds him hiding from his enemies in a wine press, the angel greets him with sarcasm: "The LORD is with you, you mighty warrior" (Judges 6:12). Yet Gideon eventually becomes a brave leader. Another example, the story of Esther, especially resonates with Moses in that she becomes a member of the ruling household of a foreign power. When the king decrees death to all Jews in his kingdom, Esther reluctantly risks her life to save her people by revealing to her husband, the king, that she herself is Jewish (Esther 4–7).

The Book of Ruth offers a powerful variation on this unlikely-hero theme. As described in Chapter 2, Ruth is a non-Israelite whose loyalty to her Israelite mother-in-law, Naomi, makes her the hero of the story. Ruth's loyalty, her willingness to risk her own well-being for the sake of Naomi, wins her the affection of an Israelite man named Boaz; they get married, and Ruth gives birth to a child. The other women laud Ruth to Naomi in terms that were radical enough for their patriarchal culture: "your daughter-in-law … is more to you than seven sons" (Ruth 4:15). Yet the real kicker is still to come. Ruth's son is named Obed, which sounds unremarkable enough until this line: Obed "became the father of Jesse, the father of David" (Ruth 4:17). This family lineage must have made spines tingle among the story's first hearers. The narrative immediately repeats the same genealogy in a slightly longer version, as if to reassure its reader that it is indeed making what would have seemed a shocking claim: Ruth, a non-Israelite, is the great-grandmother of David, the greatest king of Israel.

The story implies that her exemplary loyalty earned Ruth a rightful place in this royal lineage despite that she was an outsider. Is it any wonder that the Gospel of Matthew claims Ruth by name as an ancestor of Jesus in its otherwise male-dominated genealogy (Matthew 1:5)? The Gospels stake the authority of their ironic Messiah on this biblical theme of unlikely heroes and outsiders-made-insiders. They implicitly invoke the story of Ruth when the prophet John the Baptist admonishes his listeners, "Do not presume to say to yourselves, 'We have Abraham as our ancestor'; for I tell you, God is able from these stones to raise up children to Abraham"

(Matthew 3:8–9). John's statement also resonates with the prophet Ezekiel's vision of a multitude of dry bones transformed into human beings and brought to life by God's power (Ezekiel 37). Once again, such New Testament claims present themselves as more traditional than radical, reaffirming more than departing from biblical precedents.

DISCOVERING GOD AMONG THE OUTSIDERS: CONVERSIONS AND MIRACLES

At the same time, these stories of unexpected reversals retain a genuinely radical edge in the sense that they aim at more than mere surprise. They seem designed to challenge readers, to suggest a potential shift in perspective just as the characters in these stories typically experience a shift in their own perspectives. Moses, for example, imagines himself to be an outsider who must hide from Pharaoh. In the desert, however, he begins to discover that he is in fact the ultimate insider, the spokesperson of God (Exodus 3–4). Elijah likewise flees to the wilderness from the evil King Ahab and his conniving wife, Jezebel. At first, Elijah feels sorry for himself, complaining that he is the only faithful Israelite. Like Moses, however, he unexpectedly encounters God in the wilderness (as described in Chapter 1) and learns that he is not alone. God is with him, and seven thousand other faithful Israelites, as well; together, they will prevail against their enemies (1 Kings 19).

Moses' change in perspective is sufficiently radical that it might arguably be considered a conversion. After all, Moses initially neglects the most central Hebrew tradition of his era: he does not circumcise his son until after his encounter with God in the desert (Exodus 4:24–6). In keeping with the idea that the radical can also be traditional, the ancient Hebrew word for conversion (transliterated *shub* or *sub*) literally means "return" or "turn back," which suggests that to convert is to embrace not a new truth but an old one. This is how the Bible depicts Moses when he undertakes a life-changing new devotion to God. The story reminds us that this God is the God of Moses' ancient forebears, Abraham, Isaac, and Jacob (Exodus 3:6).

Perhaps the most famous conversion in the Bible is Paul's (who is also called Saul). At first, he self-righteously persecutes the followers of Jesus, confident that he knows the only true way to be faithful to God. Yet it turns out that he is metaphorically blind to the truth. Once he discovers that the people he considered outsiders are actually God's insiders, he becomes literally blind for three days as if to drive home the irony of the reversal (Acts 9).

Today, the idea of being "born again" is one of the well-known biblical metaphors for this kind of change in perspective. Jesus challenges a religious leader, Nicodemus, to make sense of the apparent paradox that a grown man must be "born again" in order to enter the kingdom of God (John 3:1–15). Nicodemus struggles: "How can anyone be born after having grown old?" The paradox helps represent the extent of the perspectival shift Jesus urges: like Paul, Nicodemus must learn to see differently in order to understand "heavenly things."

One way to explain the tendency in such stories for the insider (Paul or Nicodemus) to be humbled, or for the supposed outsider to come out on top, as it were, is to remember that the Bible generally casts all people as sinners. If the human condition is to be exiled from Eden, then the perspective of the outcast (often symbolized by the desert or wilderness but also by social and political powerlessness) offers a clearer and potentially truer sense of reality. It is no accident that prophets called by God in the Bible often protest at first that they are unworthy of the job. That humble sense of themselves is precisely what makes them worthy, ironically enough (e.g., Exodus 3:11, Isaiah 6:5, Jeremiah 1:6, and Ezekiel 1:28). The Bible frequently suggests that all people are prone to error and self-deception, so it makes sense that many of its stories depict characters being challenged to question their assumptions and consider alternative perspectives.

The Bible often dramatizes such perspectival shifts by pairing redemptive miracles with destructive ones. According to Revelation, Eden will be restored in the form of a New Jerusalem only after horrific devastation and calamities. The Passover miracle and the parting of the Red Sea likewise entail both destruction and liberation, as do the stories of the conquest of Canaan such as the miraculous fall of Jericho (Joshua 6). The parting of the Red Sea repeats the story of Noah and the flood: God saves Noah and the Israelites and guides them to a new beginning (much as God parts the waters in Genesis 1:6–10 to create Earth and Sky), but the lives of many others are lost in the process (Genesis 6–9 and Exodus 14). The ritual of baptism has traditionally been understood as enacting a similar two-part transformation whereby participants symbolically die (as if by drowning) in order to be resurrected in a cleansed or purified state (Romans 6:3–4). This echoes the central miracle of the New Testament, the resurrection of Jesus, which entails the torture and execution of an innocent man.

In *The Golden Bough* (1890), Scottish anthropologist James Frazer suggests that something quite similar to this two-part miracle can be found in a variety of cultures. In his view, the biblical story of Jesus' death and resurrection is typical of mythic efforts to control the seasonal cycle of birth, death, and rebirth seen in nature. In many such myths, a divine being such as a god or king dies (after the harvest), remains dead for a time (during winter), and then gets reborn (in the spring). Frazer's thesis influenced such literary works as T. S. Eliot's *The Waste Land* (1922) and William Butler Yeats's "Sailing to Byzantium" (1928), among many others.

Still more authors have been influenced by an older interpretation of the Bible's destructive recreation miracles as dramatizing a shift in perspective—a kind of conversion in which an old way of thinking must be destroyed in order to create a new one. Jesus goes so far as to say that he is glad about the death of his friend, Lazarus, because when Jesus brings him back to life, that miracle will help others believe that Jesus is the Messiah (John 11:15). In other words, the perspectival shift from doubt to belief in this story depends on and even seems to justify the suffering of Lazarus as well as his family and friends. Similarly, Jesus insists to his disciples that he must suffer and be killed; when Peter objects, Jesus rebukes him harshly: "Get behind me, Satan!" (Matthew 16:21–3). Peter must change his perspective, as Jesus explains: "you are setting your mind not on divine things but on human things" (Matthew 16:23).

In keeping with the discussion in Chapter 1 of how the Bible uses apparent paradoxes to represent divine transcendence, Jesus offers a paradoxical explanation for why he must die: "those who want to save their life will lose it, and those who lose their life for my sake will find it" (Matthew 16:25). Some see an easy interpretation here: you must be willing to lose your mortal life in order to gain eternal life. That is certainly plausible, but Jesus uses the same word, *life*, on both sides of the "equation," so to speak. Moreover, the easy interpretation potentially poses the same problem Satan poses to God in the Book of Job (discussed in Chapter 3): take away Job's prosperity, "and he will curse you to your face" (Job 1:11). If the equation is simply about personal gain, then it leaves out the kind of unselfish trust and *chesed* or *agape* (discussed in Chapter 2) that is repeatedly championed throughout the Bible—in contemporary English, it is usually translated *love*. Read as a unified whole, the Bible insists that God wants people to love him (e.g., Deuteronomy 6:5, and Matthew 22:34–40). An easy calculus of personal gain (being willing to follow Jesus only because it means swapping your mortal life for eternal life) sounds more like self-interest than love of God. The Book of Job suggests that God wants people to be motivated by something more than self-interest. The easy calculus of personal gain also poses problems for how to interpret other biblical stories such as the Akedah, Abraham's near-sacrifice of Isaac (discussed in Chapter 3). A personal-gain interpretation would cast Abraham as a sociopath willing to murder an innocent boy in the name of his own self-interest. Indeed, some do interpret the Akedah this way! Yet traditional religious interpretations see it differently.

One traditional interpretation holds that a shift in perspective, a conversion, is necessary in order to appreciate the "something more" at stake in these stories—something difficult to define that may be articulable only indirectly, especially in figurative ways that today would be considered literary. The outsider and outcast constitute two such figurative representations (which is not to say that these representations bear no literal significance), as do destructive recreation miracles. Some contend that modern readers tend to wrestle less with the idea of a crucified Messiah than with the question of whether miracles are possible, whereas the people depicted in the Bible tend to wrestle less with the possibility of miracles than with the question of what kind of power reversal is implied by a shepherd-king or crucified Messiah. (Such wrestling is implicit in two different portrayals of how Jesus feels about his own impending death: in Matthew 26:39 he wishes he could avoid it, whereas in John 12:27 he embraces it.) If the destructive recreation miracles represent conversion-like shifts in perspective, then the two questions might not be so different from each other.

THE LEGACY OF VALUING THE OUTSIDER PERSPECTIVE

Torah ends with the Israelites still in the wilderness, close to but not yet arrived in the promised land. The Christian Bible, by contrast, concludes with a vision of Eden restored (as discussed in

Chapter 1). While that vision is presented as something expected but not yet achieved—not unlike the promised land at the end of Deuteronomy—most Christian traditions teach that Jesus already achieved forgiveness and reconciliation through his death and resurrection. This has been described as an "already-not-yet" tension in Christian theology, with one side or the other sometimes receiving greater emphasis: sin and death have already been conquered but are not yet eradicated. Post-biblical Jewish history has tended to reinforce the outsider perspective of those still in the wilderness, as Jews have been persecuted for centuries and have lived predominantly in the Diaspora (outside of Israel among non-Jewish peoples). Post-biblical Christian history, by contrast—since approximately CE 313 when the Roman Emperor Constantine decriminalized Christianity—has tended to reinforce the insider perspective of the already saved, as Christianity became intertwined with various dominant political powers in Europe and, later, its colonies.

Sometimes called *triumphalism*, this already-saved sense of being history's consummate insiders—of being the ultimate winners in God's battle against evil—has helped create morally troubling but artistically rich tensions around the question of hypocrisy in Christian cultures. Christian political authorities have invoked the Bible in their defense, but so have dissenters and radicals who claimed a biblical outsider perspective and charged the insiders (whether implicitly or explicitly) with hypocrisy, much as Jesus frequently uses the word *hypocrites* to criticize religious authorities in the Gospel of Matthew. The past few centuries have witnessed such invocations of the Bible on both sides of debates over slavery, women's rights, colonization, religious toleration, and child labor laws. The Bible continues to be invoked on both sides of similar debates today such as those concerning sexuality and gender identity.

> Then they also will answer, "Lord, when was it that we saw you hungry or thirsty or a stranger or naked or sick or in prison, and did not take care of you?" Then he will answer them, "Truly I tell you, just as you did not do it to one of the least of these, you did not do it to me." (Matthew 25:44–5)

Influential twentieth-century thinkers such as Martin Buber and Emmanuel Levinas argue that encounters with another human being as *other*, as an outsider, should be considered nothing less than foundational for philosophy—indeed, for thinking about what it means to be human. The "Beat generation," mid-twentieth-century American authors such as Allen Ginsburg, Jack Kerouac, and William S. Burroughs, articulated a literary vision that resonated with thinkers like Buber and Levinas. Beat writers directed their readers' attention toward the outcast, alienated, and downtrodden *other* as not only "beaten down" but also "beatific," spiritually blessed, in keeping with the Beatitudes in which Jesus blesses the poor, the hungry, and the oppressed (Luke 6) as well as Old Testament prophets such as Isaiah (quoted above). Thus Ginsberg's *Howl* (1956) at once mourns for and celebrates those who, despite but also because of their poverty and social alienation, become "angelheaded hipsters burning for the ancient heavenly connection to the starry dynamo."

The Beat generation was influenced by earlier literary articulations of the biblical insider-outsider tension, especially the work of Percy Shelley and William Blake (discussed in Chapters 1 and 3) as well as other eighteenth- and nineteenth-century poets who later came to be known as Romantics. The Romantics embraced the biblical-outsider convention that depicts truth as more easily perceived apart from the comforts of human civilization. In the Bible, people go off into the wilderness or desert to encounter God; the Romantics headed for the Alps. That might sound as though they opted for a suspiciously fashionable version of symbolic nearness to heaven (as with Mount Sinai, Jacob's ladder, and other biblical stories that associate God with great heights)—that is, unless you know that before the eighteenth century most Europeans thought of the high Alps as a desolate, dangerous, and distinctly unfashionable wilderness. At that time, the Alps were not at all the sublime embodiment of grandeur that the Romantics helped teach most of us today to see. In this vein, the Romantics contributed to the widespread modern notion of the artist as an alienated prophet-like truth-teller, the kind of person who is not one of society's insiders but an outsider, valued because of her eccentric otherness. (By contrast, older definitions held the artist to be an intellectual or—older still—an artisan, a skilled craftsperson.)

The Romantics also contributed to an idealized notion of childhood, which resonated with the New Testament injunction to "become like children" (Matthew 18:3). In its original context, this statement most likely commended a shift in perspective from insider to outsider—commended humility in the sense of being lowly, not proud, as children occupied an especially powerless and vulnerable position in first-century Palestine. As with the Alps, however, the Romantics helped teach us to associate such outsider perspectives with deep truths. William Wordsworth hailed the child in biblical terms as a "mighty prophet" in his *Ode: Intimations of Immortality from Recollections of Early Childhood* (1807). Many people now tend to think of childhood in at least slightly Romantic terms as an age of innocence, wonder, and even special insight. Certainly such Romantic views of childhood, like the Romantics' views of nature, have influenced a wide range of twentieth- and twenty-first-century authors, often inspiring such authors (whether consciously or not) to adopt and adapt the biblical themes and imagery that inspired the Romantics.

DECONSTRUCTING BIBLICAL HIERARCHIES

When it comes to contemporary literature, the biblical insider-outsider tension resonates provocatively with literary representations of the voices and experiences of marginalized and oppressed groups and individuals (the final section of this chapter surveys specific examples). Perhaps this contemporary interest in exposing and countering oppression derives from the unique ways in which the world has grown smaller over the last hundred years as a result of modern technological advances in travel and communications. Perhaps it derives from a long, slow, and uneven process by which exploitative sociopolitical structures have given way in many parts of the world to at least somewhat more egalitarian structures. Perhaps these two historical narratives, which are often associated with the concept of modernity and especially the European Enlightenment, oversimplify history in ways that distract us from both new and old forms of exploitation and marginalization. Evaluating the relative merits of these three explanations lies beyond the scope of this book. In any case, it is clear that contemporary literature evinces an abiding interest in conflicts between different cultures, traditions, and worldviews—especially in how various kinds of socioeconomic hierarchies and power differentials among groups and individuals create, shape, and impede the very possibilities of representation, let alone the possibilities for living. The biblical insider-outsider tension holds special significance in this contemporary literary context.

Indeed, the Bible remains profoundly enmeshed with some of the most urgent and difficult questions of our time—those having to do not only with oppression and marginalization but also with epistemology, which is to say, questions about what constitutes sound knowledge. As discussed in the introduction to this book, twentieth-century poststructuralist theories, particularly deconstruction, constitute one influential way to conceptualize contemporary interests in questions of both marginalization and epistemology. Deconstructive reading strategies are based on the theory that all texts, including literary ones, tend to reinforce socioeconomic power hierarchies by echoing binary oppositions that distinguish insiders from outsiders; according to this theory, the meaning of texts depend on such binaries. Despite that such binaries are usually presented as unavoidable and fixed givens—as "natural"—poststructuralist theories maintain that they are artificial cultural constructions. This means, in turn, that they are unstable and potentially changeable. To deconstruct a text is to reveal the instabilities in the binary oppositions that help give it meaning. Deconstruction in this sense can be seen as a new form of a much older tradition that includes such forebears as William Blake's ironic exploration of the binaries named in the titles of his *Songs of Innocence and Experience* (1789) and *The Marriage of Heaven and Hell* (1790–3); William Shakespeare's dramatic exploration of sincerity versus deceit in *Hamlet* (c.1600); and the ironic depictions of insider-outsider binaries in the Bible itself.

The insights of this larger tradition can help explain how the Bible has served as a rallying cry for the outcast and oppressed but also as a "clobber text" used to support nationalism, racism, anti-Semitism, sexism, homophobia, slavery, the abuse of animals, and the mistreatment of people with disabilities. Like all texts, the Bible has a tendency to reinforce socioeconomic binaries that distinguish insiders from outsiders. Yet the Bible strongly lends itself to those who would use it to "flip" a particular hierarchical binary or reject it entirely because, as we have seen, so many biblical texts explicitly flip or otherwise undermine such binaries. Indeed, the story of the rise and fall of the Kingdom of Israel attests to the instability of political hierarchies: the Israelites begin as slaves in Egypt, become a powerful nation in Canaan, get exiled in Babylon, and eventually return to Jerusalem but never fully recover. On the one hand, the Bible foregrounds such instabilities. On the other, the Bible has often been seen as powerfully allied with political and religious authorities. Taken together, these two aspects of the Bible's reception history mean that it has resonated in unique ways with both sides of various conflicts between radical protest and traditional authority. Indeed, such conflicts themselves can be seen as enacting an unstable binary distinction between the terms *traditional* and *radical*.

Going further, many biblical texts exemplify the notion of *intersectionality*, a term that helps describe a complex set of phenomena that generally obtain in binary socioeconomic hierarchies. Different social identity-markers for such binaries (such as those having to do with class, race, sex, gender identity, ability, and religion) can reinforce or conflict with each other in complex ways. Put simply, the markers for various binaries do not exist independently but *intersect* with and even shape each other. Among other things, the notion of intersectionality can help us appreciate how we can be marginalized as well as privileged in different ways and in different contexts.

Thus those who are oppressed can also be oppressors—a tendency the Bible sometimes decries and sometimes reinforces. The Mosaic covenant specifically commands the Israelites to remember that they were once slaves so that, when they are powerful, they do not oppress others (e.g., Deuteronomy 24:17–22). Yet as escaped slaves, the Israelites need a land of their own but wipe out the Canaanites to get it (Joshua 6–12). Likewise as returned exiles, some of the Judean men intermarry with the local inhabitants but later abandon their "foreign" wives as well as their own children (Ezra 10). In the New Testament, the "scribes and Pharisees" suffer under Roman occupation but at the same time exclude and even do violence to the innocent (Matthew 23). While the early Christians were often considered outsiders by others, they were also perfectly capable of marginalizing each other: Paul rebukes wealthy Christians for humiliating poor Christians (1 Corinthians 11:20–2). Early Christianity developed in what some scholars describe as a multicultural context—a situation rife with social tensions and inequalities. Some New Testament writings reinforce those inequalities, especially the marginalization of women and slaves (1 Timothy 2:11–15, Ephesians 5:22–4 and 6:5–8, and 1 Peter 2:18).

> The eye cannot say to the hand, "I have no need of you," nor again the head to the feet, "I have no need of you." On the contrary, the members of the body that seem to be weaker are indispensable, and those members of the body that we think less honorable we clothe with greater honor, and our less respectable members are treated with greater respect; whereas our more respectable members do not need this. But God has so arranged the body, giving the greater honor to the inferior member, that there may be no dissension within the body, but the members may have the same care for one another. If one member suffers, all suffer together with it; if one member is honored, all rejoice together with it. (1 Corinthians 12:21–6)

Other New Testament writings resonate with contemporary insights about marginalization in that they specifically use the language of binary oppositions such as wisdom / foolishness, strength / weakness, and honor / dishonor, flipping them in order to undermine them and thereby urge humility rather than self-righteous pride (e.g., 1 Corinthians 1:18–31). Paul commends a sense of being spiritually equal despite apparent disparities: "There is no longer Jew or Greek, there is no longer slave or free, there is no longer male and female; for all of you are one in Christ Jesus" (Galatians 3:28).

As noted in Chapter 2, one of Paul's most influential images represents the Christian community as a body made up of different parts, all of which are necessary for the body as a whole to function—necessary not *despite* but rather *because of* their differences (see inset). The image resonates with a tension evident in modern pluralistic ideals of community: how can we foster both diversity and unity, resisting compulsory conformity and divisive factionalism at the same time? The exclusionary insider-versus-outsider narratives in Joshua and Ezra (noted above) might reflect rather extreme forms of anti-assimilation, but they might also help explain how Judaism survived centuries of exile and oppression.

The Bible's reception history echoes these ways in which certain biblical texts pointedly undermine socioeconomic hierarchies even while other biblical texts reinforce them. Scholars such as R. S. Sugirtharajah provide illuminating examples by documenting the instability of the Bible's role in British imperialism, particularly in the colonization of various indigenous peoples (such scholarship is an example of postcolonial studies, an academic field that explores the history and contemporary legacy of imperialism and colonization). In the nineteenth century, for example, the Bible was touted in British colonies as "the book your Emperor reads," the ultimate political as well as religious authority. Yet colonial subjects sometimes treated the Bible with subversive disrespect, using its pages to wrap cigars and sweetmeats, among other things. Sometimes the Bible was used with greater respect but in ways church authorities likely considered the wrong kind of respect—as a charm to protect one from bullets or to ward off sharks, or as a kind of spell to get rid of household pests such as mice and rats. (European folk traditions include similarly unorthodox uses of the Bible.)

One particularly destructive effect of the Bible among colonized peoples was the way in which its uses promoted the idea that a book— a printed, fixed text—was more authoritative than the oral traditions colonizers typically sought to undermine or even discredit. The Bible was thus used to help destabilize the authority of indigenous oral cultures and traditions. Many oral religious traditions among the peoples colonized by the British once embraced various degrees of open-endedness and changeability, according to Sugirtharajah, but under the influence of colonial rule they came to adopt the more fixed and even absolutist sense of authority associated with the Bible as a printed text. In this case, the distinction between print and oral transmission is especially ironic because the central story of the New Testament (and probably much of Hebrew scripture, as well) originated in oral traditions. Jesus never wrote anything that survived. The New Testament was not even written in Aramaic, which was undoubtedly Jesus' native language: it was written in Greek. Moreover, any English Bible is only a translation of a copy of an original, since all the original documents are lost to us.

Furthermore, if the Bible is viewed as a collection of fragments (as described in Chapter 1), the notion of the Bible as a fixed text becomes all the more uncertain. Various texts that were originally created in contexts that are largely lost to us were later appropriated by people in different contexts. That is to say, most scholars believe that Hebrew scripture was created from successive editing and re-editing of earlier texts. Much later, Christians slowly created their own additional scripture, which came to be known as the New Testament. They also continued to claim Hebrew scripture, which therefore came to be known as the Old Testament—once again reframing and thus altering the meaning of the older texts, just as earlier generations had done before them. Later still, Christian history attests to vehement and sometimes violent disagreements about how to interpret key biblical texts, leading to different traditions within Christianity that subscribe to different interpretations of the Bible and its authority.

Again, these interpretive instabilities in the Bible's reception history, as well as the unstable insider / outsider binaries foregrounded in many biblical texts, seem only to have increased the Bible's relevance to imaginative literature in the twentieth and twenty-first centuries. The remainder of this chapter surveys examples of literary works that allude to these aspects of the Bible.

OTHER VOICES, OTHER SOURCES IN CONTEMPORARY LITERATURE

American author John Steinbeck's *The Grapes of Wrath* (1939) invokes the Bible to help champion the often-maligned people who were forced to flee Oklahoma during the 1930s drought known as the Dust Bowl. Undermining a binary rich-versus-poor sense of socioeconomic class, Steinbeck casts the "Okies" (a derogatory name for these Oklahomans) as the Israelites fleeing Egypt for the promised land of Canaan—in this case, California—which turns out to be a "mirage," as H. Kelly Crockett argues. The Californians greet the Oklahomans with such contempt and malice that the land of milk and honey becomes just another wilderness of hardships.

James Baldwin's *Go Tell It on the Mountain* (1953) similarly invokes the Exodus story but in a way that self-consciously positions itself as an inheritor and continuation of the rich cultural history of African Americans refiguring the Bible in works of art (especially the Exodus story of freedom from slavery). Suffused with biblical allusions, the novel creates a complex interlocking series of binary oppositions— rich versus poor, white versus black, men versus women, religion versus art, spiritual versus sexual, and straight versus queer—building the tensions within and among these various binaries until, during the protagonist's religious conversion, he envisions the destructive-yet-recreative collapse of such binary distinctions.

Whereas Baldwin's novel especially alludes to the Book of Revelation, Jean Rhys's *Wide Sargasso Sea* (1966) draws on the Genesis story of Eden, painting nineteenth-century Jamaica as an Eden "after the fall," Heather Walton argues—an Eden defined by binary colonial relationships between England and the Caribbean, whites and blacks, men and women, and wealth and poverty. Rhys, who was born in Dominica, associates the Bible with the oppressed outsiders in these binary relationships, but she also embraces "the fallen state," according to Walton: she invokes the Bible in ways that rebel against the denial maintained by the powerful members of society who try to pretend that sin never entered the garden and that everything is perfect.

Combining Edenic imagery with a conversion narrative, Alice Walker's *The Color Purple* (1982) describes a transformation at once spiritual and sexual through which the protagonist comes to realize that "the color purple"—of wildflowers "in a field somewhere"—can intimate the presence of God (178). Walker depicts this spiritual conversion as gradually prompting the protagonist to question conventional hierarchies of class, race, gender, and sexuality. It also prompts her to learn how to tell her own story.

While many literary works that focus on gay, lesbian, or queer themes invoke the Bible in ways that resonate with *The Color Purple* (see the suggestions for further reading at the end of this chapter), some such works take the kind of postmodern approach exemplified in Jeanette Winterson's *Oranges Are Not the Only Fruit* (1985). Winterson's novel foregrounds the Bible as a key intertext, titling its eight chapters after the first eight books of the Bible. Yet it also presents fairytales as intertexts, interweaving original fairytales with its central narrative in ways that associate the fairy tales with biblical stories and thereby implicitly undermine a traditional sense of the Bible's authority. Widely considered a *Bildungsroman* (a novel about a character's formative psychological growth) or a *Künstlerroman* (a Bildungsroman about an artist), *Oranges* is a story about storytelling, like *The Color Purple*, but with a more distinctly postmodern flavor.

Another story about storytelling, Leslie Marmon Silko's *Ceremony* (1977), invokes the Bible as a significant but minor intertext, not a source or key but rather an emblem of a larger European tradition that achieves significance only as it resonates with the novel's key intertexts: indigenous American spiritual traditions. Scholars have pointed out the novel's parallels with the Fisher King legends (famously analyzed by folklorist Jessie Weston), which echo biblical depictions of sin as a cause of drought and famine (e.g., Deuteronomy 11:13–17 and Jeremiah 14:1–12). Yet Jeff Karem contends that these parallels in *Ceremony* should be understood as subordinated to and given significance by the indigenous Laguna traditions that more deeply inform the novel's formal and thematic structure. The novel represents stories as ceremonies, which it defines first and foremost by Laguna traditions.

Ceremony implicitly reminds us that we can deconstruct the very notion of the Bible as an origin or source of themes, images, and plot conventions in later works of literature. The Bible may resonate with a poem, play, or story in a way that suggests a process far more complicated than a simple one-way model of influence would allow. As noted in the introduction, the source of a particular biblical allusion or thematic resonance might be less the Bible itself than some part of its reception history (such as a King Arthur legend). In some cases, an author might allude to the Bible not as a source but because it resonates with themes, images, or plot conventions that originated in other cultural and spiritual traditions. Indeed, certain literary texts represent the Bible itself as an insider-turned-outsider.

SUMMARY

- The Bible often casts unlikely heroes performing unexpected kinds of heroism. Jesus is a paradigmatic example; additional examples include Moses, Ruth, David, and Paul.
- Such stories tend to subvert conventional human expectations in ironic ways that represent a sense of distinction between human and divine perspectives. These stories thereby imply the need for what can be termed *conversion*: a change in how human beings see the world.
- Biblical accounts of miracles sometimes have a two-part structure: first destruction, then recreation or redemption. These destructive recreations can be seen as dramatizing the conversion process whereby the old is destroyed to create a new beginning.

- Stories of conversion and miraculous recreation highlight the instability of socioeconomic insider-outsider binaries, typically by valuing outsiders and showing how someone can "flip" from one "side" of the binary to the other.
- The biblical insider-outsider tension resonates with the Bible's reception history, which evinces similar tensions.
- This aspect of the Bible and its reception history helps explain the Bible's relevance to representations of marginalized voices—one of the defining concerns of contemporary literature.

QUESTIONS FOR DISCUSSION

1   Have you ever experienced a change in perspective so extensive as to constitute a changed worldview? If so, how would you tell the story of that experience? Does your own story resonate with any similar stories in the Bible or in imaginative literature?

2   Does one or more of the miracles described in the Bible seem particularly troubling or inspiring to you? Why?

3   Do you have any favorite works of literature that focus on issues of socioeconomic marginalization and privilege? Do any of these works allude to or resonate with the Bible?

4   Do you identify with any socioeconomically marginalized or privileged groups? How do you think your experiences of being marginalized and / or privileged influence your worldview? Do you see any resonance between these experiences and biblical depictions of marginalization and privilege?

5   A common sentiment goes something like this: "Despite our differences, we are really the same underneath—we are all just people at the end of the day." To what extent do you think we need to find common ground with other people in order to form trusting and respectful relationships with them? Can we form such relationships based on our differences, as well? In your view, what answers to these questions might be suggested by specific biblical texts?

SUGGESTIONS FOR FURTHER READING

Consider reading one or more of the literary and biblical texts mentioned above. For relevant Bible readings in addition to those mentioned in this chapter, try the story of Deborah and Barak (Judges 4–5). For additional literary works, try Flannery O'Connor's "Revelation" (1965), Cynthia Ozick's *The Shawl* (1989), or Ana Castillo's *So Far from God* (1993).

For relevant nonfiction works, consider the following:

Bassard, Katherine Clay. *Transforming Scriptures: African American Women Writers and the Bible*. Athens: University of Georgia Press, 2010. Bassard analyzes various ways in which African American women used the Bible to counter oppression. See also Tuire Valkeakari, *Religious Idiom and the African American Novel, 1952–1998*. Gainesville, FL: University Press of Florida, 2007.

Crockett, H. Kelly. "The Bible and *The Grapes of Wrath*." *College English* 24.3 (December 1962): 193–9. Crockett summarizes the various biblical allusions in Steinbeck's novel. See also essays by J. R. C. Perkin and Michael J. Meyer in *Literature and the Bible*, ed. David Bevan. Amsterdam and Atlanta: Rodopi, 1993, 79–118.

Frontain, Raymond-Jean, ed. *Reclaiming the Sacred: The Bible in Gay and Lesbian Literature*. New York: Harrington Park Press, 2003. This revised second edition of the 1999 collection of essays explores a range of texts including Winterson's *Oranges Are Not the Only Fruit*. See also Norman W. Jones, *Gay and Lesbian Historical Fiction: Sexual Mystery and Post-Secular Narrative*. New York: Palgrave Macmillan, 2007, especially the third chapter's discussion of *The Color Purple* and *Go Tell It on the Mountain*.

Hamlin, Hannibal, and Norman W. Jones, eds. *The King James Bible after 400 Years: Literary, Linguistic, and Cultural Influences*. Cambridge: Cambridge University Press, 2010. Essays by R. S. Sugirtharajah, Katherine Clay Bassard, and Heather Walton offer perspectives on the Bible in postcolonial studies, African American literature, and feminist literature, respectively.

Karem, Jeff. "Keeping the Native on the Reservation: The Struggle for Leslie Marmon Silko's *Ceremony*." *American Indian Culture and Research Journal* 25.4 (2001): 21–34. Karem interprets the biblical influences in *Ceremony* as part of the novel's complex engagement with European traditions.

Ostriker, Alicia S. *Feminist Revision and the Bible*. Oxford: Blackwell Publishers, 1993. This is a useful starting point for exploring feminist scholarship on the Bible's literary legacy. See also Amy Benson Brown, *Rewriting the Word: American Women Writers and the Bible*. Westport, CT: Greenwood Press, 1999 and Jeannette King, *Women and the Word: Contemporary Women Novelists and the Bible*. New York: St. Martin's Press, 2000.

Sugirtharajah, R.S. *The Bible and Empire: Postcolonial Explorations*. Cambridge: Cambridge University Press, 2005. Sugirtharajah has authored a number of illuminating postcolonial studies of the Bible, also including *The Bible and the Third World: Precolonial, Colonial, and Postcolonial Encounters*. Cambridge and New York: Cambridge University Press, 2001. See also Frank H. Deena and Karoline Szatek, eds., *From Around the Globe: Secular Authors and Biblical Perspectives*. Lanham: University Press of America, 2007 and Roland Boer, *Last Stop Before Antarctica: The Bible and Postcolonialism in Australia*, 2nd edn. Atlanta: Society of Biblical Literature, 2008.

5

THE WORDS AND THEIR AFTERLIVES

The previous chapters focus on major themes in the Bible, only secondarily addressing formal qualities (that is, *how* the themes are conveyed) such as the use of parables that reflect on larger frame narratives; the frequent use of dramatic irony, in which the reader knows more than some characters do; a strong emphasis on intertextuality (repetitions of themes, plots, and imagery); the extensive use of figurative language (especially to describe God); sparse storytelling that provides subtle hints about characters' thoughts and emotions; and the use of ironic reversals that subvert binary insider-outsider hierarchies. These formal qualities have thus far been highlighted to help illuminate major themes and their literary legacies. This final chapter changes focus, turning away from thematic concerns to explore the most influential formal qualities of English Bible translations, especially those that have not yet been addressed. Are there such things as distinctively biblical sentences, phrases, and individual words? To what extent have imaginative literatures been influenced by this small-scale structure of the Bible?

Perhaps it should not surprise us that even the individual words, phrases, and sentence structure of the Bible have their own literary legacy. After all, the words themselves are important: in Jewish traditions, God is present in the words of Torah. Indeed, Jews refer to themselves as the People of the Book (Muslims and some Christians also use this phrase to describe themselves). In Christian traditions, God's immanence is manifest especially in Jesus. The Gospel of John figures Jesus as "the Word" of God through whom all things were created—in keeping with the account of creation in the opening of Genesis, where God uses words to speak the world into existence. In the Bible, even individual words have power.

THE GENESIS OF THE ENGLISH BIBLE: A MATTER OF LIFE AND DEATH

To understand the reception history of the small-scale structure of the Bible, it is helpful to begin with a brief history of the Bible as a text. For that, we must go back to Hebrew scripture or Tanakh, which probably achieved something close to its present shape during the first centuries of the Common Era. Yet collections of Hebrew scripture had existed for many centuries before then. One of the most influential was a third-century BCE Greek translation that came to be known as the Septuagint, so-called because it was said to have been translated by seventy scholars. Such collections did not mean that Hebrew scripture was a fixed *canon* (or rule) of texts accepted by Jewish authorities as holy scripture. The notion of a canon of scripture developed alongside the invention of the *codex*, which bound separate pages together along one edge—the forerunner of the modern book. The New Testament canon was established by the late fourth century CE, when the codex had rendered scrolls largely obsolete.

We might not look at a book and see a technological innovation, but once upon a time, it was. Prior to the first centuries of the Common Era, holy scripture existed only as collections of scrolls, which meant that the order and even possibly the inclusion or exclusion of individual "books" or scrolls was less fixed. Indeed, the Greek *Biblia* originally meant "little books." Only later did the term *Bible* come to signify one single book whose covers clearly defined which texts were included, which were excluded, and how they were ordered.

By the time of Jesus, most Jews no longer knew ancient Hebrew. In Canaan—the most common biblical name for the geographical area commonly referred to as Palestine, which roughly comprises the modern-day states of Israel and Palestine—Jews primarily spoke Aramaic, a linguistic descendant of Hebrew. Scholars therefore created what were called *Targums*, Aramaic translations or paraphrases of Hebrew scripture that often included commentaries to help render the ancient texts more intelligible to Aramaic speakers.

While Aramaic was the language spoken by Jesus and his followers, many Jews also knew a simplified version of Greek called *Koiné*. This helps explain why the New Testament was originally composed in Greek (except for a few phrases in Aramaic), and why New Testament references to Hebrew scripture generally use the Septuagint (Greek) version. In the late fourth century CE, Jerome—a talented scholar of Latin, Greek, and Hebrew—created a Latin translation of most of the Old and New Testaments, drawing on the original Hebrew as well as the Greek Septuagint for the Old Testament. Other scholars completed Jerome's work, and the full translation came to be known as the *Vulgate*, meaning "common." It was long considered to be the common or standard version of the Christian Bible because Latin was known by such a wide variety of literate peoples throughout medieval Europe. Indeed, the Vulgate served as the standard Christian version of the Bible in the West for more than a thousand years. (The Eastern Orthodox Church used a Greek version.)

In the late fourteenth century, John Wyclif's associates created the first complete English translation of the Bible. They aimed to make scripture directly accessible to English-speaking Christians who did not know Latin. Yet it would be wrong to imagine that this was a new idea: for hundreds of years before Wyclif, various scholars had translated parts of the Bible into Old English. After Wyclif, another century would pass before Martin Luther helped inspire the Protestant split from the Roman Catholic Church in what came to be known as the Reformation. One of the central tenets of the reformers—that ordinary Christians should be able to hear or read the Bible in their own native languages—motivated the Wyclifites long before Luther created his famous German translation.

By the fifteenth century, translating the Bible into English had become a risky undertaking because it could be seen as undermining the authority of the Church. Wyclif died in 1384, and less than thirty years later, translating the Bible into English was outlawed. Less than twenty years after that, Wyclif's corpse was exhumed and burned as punishment for the Wyclifite Bible. Yet copies of it survive to this day despite the fact that relatively few must have been created before they became illegal. They had to be hand-copied, after all: the printing press was not invented until more than a decade after Wyclif's corpse was desecrated. Clearly there were passionately committed partisans on both sides of the Bible-translation conflict.

William Tyndale was the next major torch-bearer on the side of the English translators, and his translation of the New Testament in 1526 became the first English New Testament produced by a printing press. Such translations were still illegal in England, so Tyndale published it on the Continent and then went on to publish translations of the Pentateuch and the Book of Jonah, as well. Before he could finish the rest of the Bible, Tyndale was accused of heresy and executed by strangulation in 1536. Then, for good measure, they burned his body. Yet Tyndale, like the Wyclifites, succeeded despite such opposition: not only do copies of Tyndale's translation survive today, but later translators esteemed his work so highly that it was used in other translations. Indeed, much of the Authorized or King James Version (KJV) of the Bible—which was published not quite a century after Tyndale's and became the dominant English translation for most of the past four hundred years—is heavily indebted to Tyndale's version.

King Henry VIII and his advisers seem to have recognized that the translation efforts could not be stopped, so he instead attempted to control them by ordering an official English translation that came to be known as the Great Bible. Published in 1539, it was based largely on the work of Tyndale but also that of John Rogers and Miles Coverdale. A former assistant of Tyndale's, Coverdale had published the first complete printed copy of the English Bible in 1535; he also published an English Psalter, a stand-alone edition of the Book of Psalms.

Despite the new availability of English Bibles, English translations soon became illegal again during Queen Mary's reign. When Elizabeth I became queen, the law changed once more, and Henry's Great Bible quickly became eclipsed in popularity by the Geneva Bible—a translation published in 1560 by English Calvinists who fled to Geneva to escape religious persecution.

While the Geneva Bible dominated English markets for roughly a century, more traditionally minded authorities continued to try to establish a less reform-oriented translation. The Bishops' Bible (1568) became the official Church of England translation during Elizabeth's reign. Later, a group of English Catholics published the Douai-Rheims Bible. Neither of these unseated the Geneva Bible; that achievement fell to the KJV, first published in 1611 by order of James I. While not immediately popular and never officially authorized by the government (according to surviving records), the KJV became the dominant English Bible within a few decades of its initial publication. It maintained that status until the 1980s when, in terms of sales, it was finally "dethroned" (as Paul C. Gutjahr describes it) by the New International Version.

How did the KJV retain its dominance for more than three centuries? There is no simple answer, but a good place to start is the story of its origin. When James I ascended the throne of England in 1603, he found himself caught in a tug-of-war between religious reformers and traditionalists—and in that era, this tension had political as well as religious significance. A new official Bible translation was urged by a leading reformer, but James seems to have accepted the idea more as an opportunity to bring the two sides together rather than to choose one over the other. The KJV was thus created out of conflict but was designed in part to ameliorate that conflict—to hold the two sides in tension by being committed to tradition but also to consensus. It was translated by an elaborate committee structure rather than by a lone individual: six "companies" (two at Oxford, two at Cambridge, and two at Westminster) comprised approximately fifty scholars in total. These committees aimed to create not an entirely new translation but instead one that incorporated the best qualities of prior English translations, drawing on both reformist and traditionalist versions.

In this sense the KJV was born as the culmination of two centuries of English Bible translation, which suggests that its longstanding pre-eminence is due to the high quality of the work. Yet many have pointed out that it was also born out of the intimate relationship between religion and politics, and that it then "grew up," so to speak, as the adopted child of one of the most powerful empires the world has known. To some extent, its authoritative status in England and her colonies may have been due to the ways in which it became part of the self-protective machinery of state-sponsored commerce (as noted in Chapter 4).

For example, the KJV uses the word *church* (suggestive of the state-sponsored institution in that period of English history) in place of Tyndale's more democratic *congregation* (suggestive of the people). It likewise eschews both Tyndale's and the Bishops' Bible's "multitude of heavenly soldiers" who visit the shepherds after the birth of Jesus (Luke 2:13). The KJV describes them as a "heavenly host," which Stephen Prickett argues was less likely to inspire religious dissidents to take up arms in the name of God.

As a translation, the KJV possesses extensive merits but is not absolutely perfect. Over time, several revisions were deemed necessary (today, new printings of the KJV tend to use the Oxford edition of 1769, typically with updated spellings). Translations created in the last several decades benefit from a wealth of historical research that was unavailable at the beginning of the seventeenth century. Yet most of these contemporary translations attempt to clarify difficult passages by offering less literal translations of those passages, which can narrow the possible range of interpretations in ways that belie the complexities of the original sources—complexities that the KJV, by contrast, tends to reproduce more faithfully.

For example, the KJV reproduces an idiomatic Hebrew use of the verb *to know* in the story of Adam and Eve: "Adam knew Eve, his wife" (Genesis 4:1). Even though many readers today understand what it means to know another person "in the biblical sense," recent translations often clarify the meaning of this euphemism either by using a more contemporary euphemism (the Message has "Adam slept with Eve, his wife"), a more contemporary idiomatic expression (the New International Version has "Adam made love to his wife"), or a non-euphemistic explanation (the New Living Translation has "Adam had sexual relations with his wife"). As Hannibal Hamlin points out, these contemporary translations keep the reader from potentially recognizing that *to know* as a euphemism for sexual intercourse resonates provocatively with the tree of the *knowledge* of good and evil—as well as with Adam and Eve's coming to *know* that they are naked as a result of eating the fruit of the tree (Genesis 2–3). (For recent translations of Hebrew scripture that convey this kind of wordplay, see the suggestions for further reading at the end of this chapter.)

Today, readers can choose from a wealth of different Bible translations, and none of them dominates the way the KJV once did (see at the end of this volume "A note on English Bible translations" for a brief overview of some popular translations). Even if you strongly prefer a contemporary translation, however, it is still worth knowing about the KJV—not only because of its influence on language and literature but also because of its influence on later English Bibles. That influence has been so profound that when judging the relative merits of contemporary translations, well-informed readers often ask whether the translation tries to maintain the characteristic sound and phrasing of the KJV or whether it eschews that tradition in favor of more contemporary phrasing.

Two other commonly asked questions are, first, does the translation reflect more of a "conservative" or a "liberal" interpretation? For example, does it use translation options that reinforce a sense of harmony between the Old and New Testaments (which is often considered conservative), or does it opt for gender-inclusive language where possible (often considered liberal)? Second, did the translators use a literal, word-for-word approach ("formal equivalence") or a more interpretive, thought-for-thought approach ("functional equivalence," which twentieth-century linguist Eugene Nida called "dynamic equivalence")?

That last question helps explain what is distinctive about the KJV. Much of what defines the characteristic sound of the KJV is the translators' commitment to create, as much as possible, a word-for-word translation of the ancient texts. The KJV thus ended up preserving some of the characteristics of the ancient Hebrew and Greek, which, over the course of the KJV's four centuries, created an indelible impression on the English language as well as on imaginative literature.

HOW TO SOUND LIKE THE BIBLE

The KJV has a fairly uniform sound. Despite the translators' goal of being faithful to the original Hebrew, Greek, and Aramaic source texts, this uniformity actually distorts some of those originals. Stephen Prickett calls it "the King James Steamroller": it flattens out the stylistic differences among its various sources and thereby creates a false sense that the Bible speaks in just one uniform voice. While this steamroller effect arguably detracts from the translation's accuracy, it has also been a strength, contributing to what many consider the beauty of the KJV's consistently stately rhythms. It was designed to possess this kind of sound: the six companies of scholars tested their translations by reading them aloud, perhaps because they expected that the final result would be read aloud regularly in churches. Their success can be seen in how the KJV created a sense of "Church English"—the slowly measured rhythm many people associate with formal worship and prayer.

A crucial aspect of this sound is that it was deliberately old-fashioned, as if meant to seem like a voice from the past. Even in 1611, the language of the KJV was not that of ordinary speech but already had a slightly archaic feel. It used older forms of English that had largely fallen out of use, such as *thee, thou*, and the *-eth* suffix (as in Luke 22:21, "Behold, the hand of him that *betrayeth* me is with me on the table"). The archaic sound of this language has only increased over time.

Thanks to the KJV, *thee* and *thou* now sound formal to most modern ears because we tend to associate them with formal Church English. Yet these words originally had the opposite connotation: they were used as informal ways to address well-known friends and family members. By contrast, *you* was appropriate for more formal situations.

While *thee, thou*, and the *–eth* suffix now sound even more strange and archaic than they did in 1611, other features of the KJV now sound less so. The translators' word-for-word approach meant that they often reproduced ancient idiomatic expressions and grammatical constructions literally, creating new English expressions unfamiliar to non-scholarly audiences in the early seventeenth century. Today, however, many of these expressions have become familiar staples of the English language. Some still sound at least a bit strange and archaic because you might know them only as they appear in the Bible (if at all), in which case they probably sound biblical. Others have become such an integral part of the English language that they sound English—we typically forget their biblical origins.

Take, for example, the following common English sayings, all of which were inspired by or directly quote from English translations of the Bible:

> "a drop in the bucket" (Isaiah 40:15)
> "a fly in the ointment" (Ecclesiastes 10:1)

"a labor of love" (1 Thessalonians 1:3)
"a man after his own heart" (1 Samuel 13:14)
"by the skin of my teeth" (Job 19:20)
"den of thieves" (Mark 11:17)
"far be it from me" (1 Samuel 20:9)
"fell flat on his face" (Numbers 22:31)
"from time to time" (Ezekiel 4:10)
"lick the dust" (Psalm 72:9)
"no respecter of persons" (Acts 10:34)
"put words in his mouth" (Exodus 4:15)
"rise and shine" (Isaiah 60:1)
"sick to death" (2 Kings 20:1)
"sour grapes" (Ezekiel 18:2, Jeremiah 31:29-30)
"stand in awe" (Psalm 4:4)
"the land of the living" (Psalm 27:13)
"the last gasp" (2 Maccabees 7:9)
"the salt of the earth" (Matthew 5:13)
"to pour out your heart" (Lamentations 2:19)

Likewise, the following grammatical features of ancient Hebrew influenced imaginative literatures as well as English language usage more broadly. Some of these features now sound biblical (depending on a given reader's level of familiarity with the Bible). Some simply sound archaic and formal (especially if a given reader is unfamiliar with the Bible):

- The KJV forms possessives by using a "noun + of + noun" construction (e.g., "the face of God") because ancient Hebrew does not form possessives by using an apostrophe as English typically does (e.g., "God's face"). While there was nothing particularly formal about possessives in ancient Hebrew, English speakers now tend to think of this biblical construction of possessives as more formal than the typical English construction.
- The KJV also tends to use "noun + of + noun" constructions instead of "adjective + noun" ones: "men of strength" instead of "strong men" (Isaiah 5:22); "altar of stone" instead of "stone altar" (Exodus 20:25); or "man of God" (which appears dozens of times, as in Deuteronomy 33:1) instead of "godly man" (which appears only once, in Psalm 12:1). Some argue that

"noun + adjective" constructions in English derive from this biblical influence (e.g., "gardens bright" in the opening stanza of S. T. Coleridge's *Kubla Khan*).

- Instead of using typical English superlative constructions (e.g., "the greatest king"), the KJV again follows the ancient Hebrew by using a "noun + of + noun" construction such as "the king of kings" (Ezra 7:12) or "the song of songs" (Song of Solomon 1:1).

- Instead of the typical English subject-verb-object construction, the KJV often reproduces a Hebraism by which the object of the verb comes before the subject, as David Norton points out: "as for his judgments, they have not known them" (Psalm 147:20) rather than "they have not known his judgments."

- Ancient Hebrew did not use as many subordinating conjunctions as English commonly uses to mark one clause as independent and the other as dependent, such as *although*, *nevertheless*, *therefore*, *until*, *whether*, and *while* (to name just a few). By contrast with such hypotactic grammatical constructions (typical of English), ancient Hebrew favored paratactic constructions: it used the Hebrew connective transliterated *waw* as a coordinating conjunction like the English *and*, which the KJV translators reproduced to an extent that sounds quite unusual in English. For those unfamiliar with grammatical terms, this explanation might sound confusing until you hear the opening lines of the KJV with the frequent use of *and* italicized:

In the beginning God created the heaven and the earth. *And* the earth was without form, and void, *and* darkness was upon the face of the deep. *And* the Spirit of God moved upon the face of the waters. *And* God said, "Let there be light": *and* there was light. *And* God saw the light, that it was good: *and* God divided the light from the darkness. *And* God called the light Day, and the darkness he called Night. *And* the evening and the morning were the first day.

(Genesis 1:1–5, emphasis added)

One might sum up most of the above features with the simple observation that biblical Hebrew had fewer options at its disposal—considerably fewer words than Elizabethan English possessed. This created yet another distinctive feature: writers had to repeat vocabulary and grammatical structures with slight variations for different purposes, which seems to have inspired its own kind of artistry. A single word or phrase used in a biblical text can resonate with other uses of the same or similar words and phrases elsewhere in the text; each use recalls the earlier ones, creating layered meanings by inviting associations between the various instances of the particular word or phrase. Hebrew scripture creates intentionally cumulative reiterations on this small-scale level of individual words and phrases—a sense of intra textuality that echoes the Bible's large-scale intertextuality. Once your ears become attuned to the resonance created by these self-echoing sounds in the Bible, you begin to hear how both the larger stories and individual passages hum with a kind of theme-and-variations intensity that can rise to symphonic levels of complexity.

Consider Psalm 69, which uses the image of flooding to articulate a sense of near-hopeless distress: "Save me, O God; for the waters are come in unto my soul. I sink in deep mire, where there is no standing: I am come into deep waters, where the floods overflow me. I am weary of my crying: my throat is dried: mine eyes fail while I wait for my God" (Psalm 69:1–3). As David Norton attests, these concrete images (*waters* and *floods* instead of words such as *misery* or *despair*) exemplify how ancient Hebrew vocabulary favors concrete terms over abstract ones but uses concrete images to express abstract ideas. Norton points out (drawing on the work of earlier scholars such as Ernest Renan) that the Hebrew verb meaning *to be jealous* derives from the verb *to glow*; the noun *truth* comes from the verb *to prop, to build, to make firm*; and the same word used for *self* also means *bone*. Thus concrete words such as *bone* or *build* often develop rich, multi-layered significance as they get repeated with different meanings in the same text. Robert Alter describes them as biblical "keywords"—*dust, earth, land, clay, blood, flesh, seed, fruit, lamb, gate,* and *house,* among others.

When teaching the Bible, I sometimes ask students to choose one of these keywords and research its various uses in the Bible (using a concordance or online search engine), summarizing and analyzing their findings in the form of an essay. This exercise helps illuminate the rich complexity that can be achieved through the creative repetition of seemingly simple concrete nouns.

In Psalm 69, the waters invoke not only an abstract emotion but also the creation of the earth when God separated the waters; the story of Noah and the flood; and the Exodus story about the parting of the Red Sea. Those are only the most obvious echoes. Then the Psalm itself associates these waters with tears, ironically contrasting the destructive floodwaters with the suggestion of thirst and dehydration ("my throat is dried"). This contrast foreshadows the change in tone (common to many Psalms) from desperate pleading to confident assurance that "God will save Zion" (verse 35) as the speaker's potential drowning and failing eyes (verse 3) become imaginatively transferred to his enemies: "Let their eyes be darkened," and let God "pour out thine indignation upon them" (verses 23 and 24). These sentiments help create the *chiastic* structure of the Psalm, a special kind of repetition common in biblical narrative and poetry whereby one or more statements are reversed in a self-mirroring series— e.g., statement A, statement B, then reverse-B, and reverse-A. This crossover-effect implies the existence of meaningful associations not only between A / reverse-A and B / reverse-B but also between A / B, A / reverse-B, and B / reverse-A. The Psalm thus creates a web of self-reflective repetitions.

Psalm 69 also illustrates the frequent use of *hyperbole* and *parallelism* in the Bible. Hyperbole refers to an intentional exaggeration, expressing an idea or emotion in an extreme form: "They that hate me without a cause are more than the hairs of mine head" (verse 4). While hyperbole might suggest oversimplification to some readers (on the grounds that extreme sentiments fail to capture subtler and usually more accurate gradations and shadings), ancient Hebrew often uses repetition to achieve a more subtle and complex effect even with hyperbole than you might at first imagine.

Take just two of the opening lines of Psalm 69: "I sink in deep mire, where there is no standing: I am come into deep waters, where the floods overflow me." These are hyperbolic constructions ("no standing" and "overflow me"): the speaker would presumably already be drowned and unable to speak if these extremes were taken literally. They are also an example of what eighteenth-century scholar Robert Lowth first identified as *parallelism* in Hebrew poetry, a deliberate pattern (as rhythm and rhyme are often used in Anglophone poetry) whereby each verse consists of two or more statements that work together in one of three ways (depending on the categorization scheme used). They can be *synonymous* (the second restates the first), as in the second verse of Psalm 149: "Let

Israel rejoice in him that made him: let the children of Zion be joyful in their King." They can be *synthetic* (the second builds on the first): "Let them praise his name in the dance: let them sing praises unto him with the timbrel and harp" (Psalm 149:3). Or they can be *antithetical* (the second contrasts with the first): "let the wickedness of the wicked come to an end, but establish the just" (Psalm 7:9).

The beginning of Psalm 69 uses synthetic parallelism: "I sink in deep mire," and "I am come into deep waters." The combined water and earth imagery implicitly reverses the creation account in Genesis, suggesting that the mire or muddy ground symbolizes the threat that the speaker will be unmade. Creation required separating the water from the ground: by God's power, the waters were "gathered together unto one place" in order to make "dry land" (Genesis 1:9). Later, God created Adam from the dry "dust of the ground" (Genesis 2:7). Thus the hyperbole in Psalm 69 is even more grandly exaggerated than might at first appear. By echoing key imagery from Genesis, the opening of the Psalm grounds the speaker's lament in a sense of dependence on God: God made him, and God can unmake him. This sense of dependence foreshadows the later reversal of mood to one of hope and trust that God will not unmake the speaker but will save him. In other words, the parallelism suggests that these hyperbolic laments serve not to erase subtlety but rather to create it, dramatizing the later change in mood and suggesting that the speaker trusts God even in despair. (A more famous example of this characteristic reversal is Psalm 22, which begins, "My God, my God, why hast thou forsaken me?" Jesus speaks these words on the cross in Mark 15:34, quoting a Psalm that ends reassuringly: "All the ends of the world shall remember and turn unto the LORD: and all the kindreds of the nations shall worship before thee.")

Even when not using the formal parallelism found in Hebrew poetry, biblical narratives often achieve a similar effect through a less structured use of cumulative enumerations. Recall, for example, the story of David and Absalom (discussed in Chapter 2), specifically the passage in which Joab admonishes King David in a stately rhythm that carries prophetic undertones:

> Thou hast shamed this day the faces of all thy servants, which this day have saved thy life, and the lives of thy sons and of thy daughters, and the lives of thy wives, and the lives of thy concubines, in that thou lovest

thy enemies, and hatest thy friends. ... For this day I perceive, that if Absalom had lived, and all we had died this day, then it had pleased thee well.

(2 Samuel 19:5–6)

The sentences are composed of rather brief phrases (the many commas visibly mark this pacing), and the cumulative enumeration ("lives of thy sons ... daughters ... wives ... concubines") and pairing of ironic reversals ("lovest they enemies, and hatest thy friends") serve to keep the rhythm slow and measured while also building tension through the repetition of closely-linked themes and variations. Joab's final ironic accusation thus comes as the climax to the drumbeat intensity of his speech: if all David's loyal soldiers had died and his enemy had lived, "it had please thee well."

The prophetic undertones of this speech (not only the meaning but also the sound) then take a new turn, rising more clearly to the surface as he seems to bear witness against David on behalf of God himself: "I swear by the LORD, if thou go not forth ... that will be worse unto thee than all the evil that befell thee from thy youth until now" (2 Samuel 19:7). The KJV's archaic vocabulary might at first seem to be the most distinctive feature of the speech as a whole—*thee, thou, thy, doth, lovest, hatest, forth,* and *befell*—and indeed such vocabulary today sounds biblical to many ears (a sound that also seems to carry the kind of prophetic tones found in Joab's speech; I will return shortly to this prophetic quality). In addition to the vocabulary, however, the KJV also "sounds biblical" in the ways I have been describing: it reproduces the theme-and-variation sense of repetition so vital to biblical poetry and narrative.

LITERARY LEGACIES: FREE VERSE, CONCRETE IMAGERY, AND HAUNTED VOICES

Many twentieth- and twenty-first-century poets owe at least an indirect debt to the Bible to the extent that they have been inspired by the free verse of Walt Whitman. In writing *Leaves of Grass* (1855–67), Whitman hoped that his poetry would become a "new American Bible"—American especially in the sense that it would be democratically anti-hierarchical and exuberantly anti-authoritarian. He drew especially on the parallelism of the Psalms for the basic structure of his otherwise unstructured *free verse* (poetry without a regular pattern of rhyme or rhythm). For example, in "Song of Myself, 6" (1892) we see a pattern of repetition whereby each phrase or sentence gets echoed or expanded on by a second phrase or sentence:

> A child said *What is the grass?* fetching it to me with full hands;
> How could I answer the child? I do not know what it is any more than he.
> I guess it must be the flag of my disposition, out of hopeful green stuff woven.
> Or I guess it is the handkerchief of the Lord,
> A scented gift and remembrancer designedly dropped.

Whitman, in turn, was the major precursor for later generations of poets writing in free verse, as H. T. Kirby-Smith demonstrates. More than half a century after Whitman's "Song of Myself, 6," the free verse of Allen Ginsberg's *Howl* (1956) is similarly informed by Whitman's adaptation of biblical form:

> I saw the best minds of my generation destroyed by madness, starving hysterical naked,
> dragging themselves through the Negro streets at dawn looking for an angry fix,
> angelheaded hipsters burning for the ancient heavenly connection to the starry dynamo in the machinery of night,
> who poverty and tatters and hollow-eyed and high sat up smoking in the supernatural darkness of cold-water flats floating across the tops of cities contemplating jazz
> who bared their brains to Heaven under the El and saw Mohammedan angels staggering on tenement roofs illuminated.

Such free verse sometimes adopts a recognizably biblical parallelism. Elsewhere, it embraces a general sense of cumulative enumeration similar to that found in many biblical narratives such as Joab's speech from the David-and-Absalom story, quoted above (2 Samuel 19).

A great deal of twentieth- and twenty-first-century poetry resonates with the Bible in a vaguer but no less important way. This resonance can be summed up by the famous dictum of twentieth-century American poet William Carlos Williams, which helped inspire so many subsequent poets: "No ideas but in things." The

Bible's emphasis on concrete rather than abstract language took on a particularly modern cast in the twentieth century, a relevance that remains undiminished for many authors. Our language and literature continue to embrace the concrete imagery of biblical proverbs and aphorisms—brief but pithy distillations of ancient wisdom— many of which have become such a part of our language that we often fail to realize they derive from the Bible:

> "a house divided cannot stand" (Matthew 12:25)
> "a wolf in sheep's clothing" (Matthew 7:15)
> "beat your plowshares into swords" (Joel 3:10)
> "can a leopard change his spots?" (Jeremiah 13:23)
> "don't cast your pearls before swine" (Matthew 7:6)
> "don't let the sun go down on your anger" (Ephesians 4:26)
> "eat, drink, and be merry, for tomorrow we die" (Isaiah 22:12–13, 1 Corinthians 15:32)
> "fight the good fight" (1 Timothy 6:12)
> "for everything there is a season" (Ecclesiastes 3:1)
> "love of money is the root of all evil" (1 Timothy 6:10)
> "out of the mouths of babes" (Psalm 8:2, Matthew 21:16)
> "reap what you sow" (Job 4:8, Luke 19:21, Galatians 6:7)
> "straight and narrow" (Matthew 7:14)
> "the blind leading the blind" (Matthew 15:14, Luke 6:39)

These sayings live on in ways far removed from their original contexts—much like the New Testament parables or the miracle of turning water into wine, all of which favor concrete imagery over ideas. The easy-to-visualize water-to-wine miracle, for example, conveys a startling sense of transformation even if you are unfamiliar with how water and wine resonate with other biblical stories of transformation. Nor does the narrative need to specifically state that this miracle is the first of Jesus' ministry and therefore represents a much larger transformation; the story is arguably stronger without such an explanation (John 2:1–11). Similarly, the sayings above spark the imagination even without any understanding of their specifically biblical significance. Much modern and contemporary writing aims to achieve the kind of concrete, visceral impact exemplified in the Bible, as attested by one of the most often-repeated creative writing maxims: "Show, don't tell."

In addition to parallelism and concrete imagery, there is an equally modern way in which the formal aspects of the Bible have influenced certain strands of twentieth- and twenty-first-century literature. The Bible—especially the KJV—has sometimes functioned as a ghostly intertext, an ancient voice whose sounds can haunt present-day narratives in a vague yet insistent way.

For some, the Bible is a living text: traditionally minded Jews and Christians generally believe that reading and studying holy scripture in community enacts the presence of the living God (the Shekinah or, for Christians, the inspiration of the Holy Spirit). For other readers, the Bible is a dead text: over the last two hundred years there has been a considerable increase in the number of English speakers who completely reject traditional religious interpretations of the Bible. For still others, however, the Bible is not exactly a living text in the traditional religious sense but also is not exactly dead. Most such readers constitute the underappreciated denizens of various "middle grounds" between traditional religious and modern secular views. Among these readers are authors who have created some of the most influential modern and contemporary works of literature. In what follows, I focus on a few examples of such literary works that implicitly invite their readers to consider the Bible as a kind of ghost— neither dead nor alive in any simple way, speaking insistently to the present from the past in prophetic tones that are sometimes arresting, sometimes inspiring, but never perfectly clear.

There are several specifically modern ways in which the Bible can lend itself to being invoked as a ghostly sound or voice in imaginative literature. First, for modern readers familiar with the Higher Criticism (discussed in Chapter 1), the Bible can be seen as a mosaic of fragments that were edited together long ago in complex and highly subjective ways, which means they obscured the contexts and intentions of the original authors. Later, this collection of re-edited fragments was translated into English in ways that created such uniformity in the sound of the various texts ("the King James Steamroller" described above) that the differences among the original sources became even further obscured beneath the illusion of a single unified book. Yet the original fragments remain, however dimly. Their simultaneous presence-and-absence, like that of a ghost, can seem well suited to the archaic language and style of the KJV despite the steamroller effect: as contemporary English grows further removed from sixteenth- and seventeenth-century linguistic conventions, the increasingly strange and ancient sound of the KJV can seem to speak to the present from a more distant past than it did in previous centuries. Compounding that sense of distance from the Bible, modern science and technology have rendered the daily experiences and worldview described in the Bible more different from the present, more archaic, than ever before.

Virginia Woolf's *To the Lighthouse* (1927) invokes the Bible in elusive yet insistent ways that suggest this particularly modern view of ancient scripture. Tracing Woolf's beautiful and mysterious invocations of the KJV, James Wood argues that *To the Lighthouse* is "one of the most religious of modern secular English novels" because of the "ghostliness of its biblical allusions." Woolf's novel struggles with what might be described as the philosophical ghostliness of the Bible, which raises the possibility of transcendence. The novel explores this possibility especially in the context of intimate human relationships, in keeping with some of the themes outlined in Chapters 1 and 2.

Other modern and contemporary invocations of the Bible-as-ghost draw on the themes outlined in Chapters 3 and 4: the biblical allusions haunting these narratives speak more prophetically than philosophically, crying out to the present to right past wrongs like Abel's blood crying out for justice from the ground. Toni Morrison's *Beloved* (1987) offers one such invocation. Inspired by historically documented events, *Beloved* reimagines the story of a woman who, in 1856, escaped from a plantation in the southern United States where she had been enslaved. Later captured by slave catchers, she attempted to kill her four children in order to save them from being enslaved again. She succeeded in killing only one. The novel reimagines her life as a ghost story, beginning after the abolition of slavery when Sethe (the protagonist) lives as a free woman haunted by the ghost of her dead baby girl.

Beloved suggests that a ghost is an apt symbol for the haunting legacy of slavery in the U.S. because the history of African Americans is ghostly—at once there and not there. African American stories are integral to U.S. history yet have often been overlooked and avoided in white accounts of that history. As a result of the many ways in which literacy was made unavailable to slaves, there are only a small number of first-hand accounts of eighteenth- and nineteenth-century African American lives. Most of those lives are marked only by a ghostly absence from historical records, testified to only indirectly and uncertainly. *Beloved* calls attention to their voices, imaginatively laying claim to their lost stories in the spirit of Romans 9:25 (which serves as the novel's epigraph): "I will call them my people, which were not my people; and her beloved, which was not beloved."

Morrison's ghostly allusions to the Bible in *Beloved* undermine the kind of heartlessly authoritarian interpretations of the Bible that were used to help defend the practice of slavery in the nineteenth century. Indeed, the fact that people cited the Bible to help authorize such oppression renders literary invocations of the Bible potentially more powerful. By foregrounding its propensity for ironically subverting socioeconomic hierarchies, literary invocations of the Bible can help undermine the sense of authority it has lent to socioeconomic oppression. Yet *Beloved* goes further than that, casting the Bible itself as a ghostly intertext by creating vague allusions to the distinctive language and style of the KJV. It thereby implicitly suggests that the authority of the Bible itself is somehow ghostly, there but not fully graspable, something to be wrestled with but not contained or defined—not unlike the ghost of Sethe's dead baby girl, Beloved, who continues to haunt the world at the end of the novel as an uncontainable and indefinable but insistently present-yet-absent ghost.

SUMMARY

- A brief history of the textual origins of the Bible helps set the stage for a slightly-less-brief history of English Bible translations.
- Distinctive formal features of the KJV have influenced not only imaginative literatures but also the English language.
- These formal features include using ancient Hebrew idiomatic expressions; the use of noun + of + noun constructions to form possessives, adjectives, and superlatives; paratactic grammatical connections (e.g., the frequent use of *and*); favoring concrete over abstract

language; the cumulative repetition of imagery and sentiments (the most structured form of this is parallelism);
hyperbole; the use of keywords that are at once literal and
symbolic; and the tendency to favor short, pithy (aphoris-
tic) statements.

- The literary influence of these formal features—the
"sound" of the Bible—becomes especially clear in
twentieth- and twenty-first-century literatures, specifically in certain kinds of free verse, the general predilec-
tion for concrete over abstract imagery, and invocations
of the Bible as a ghostly intertext.

QUESTIONS FOR DISCUSSION

1   Based on your experience, what does the Bible sound like? Can
you write a sentence that is not in the Bible (as far as you know)
but that nevertheless sounds biblical to you?

2   In terms of your own personal interests, which of the following is most important or significant to you when it comes to
choosing a version of the Bible to read? Why? (a) The Bible's
original Hebrew, Greek, and Aramaic—you would like to learn
about the untranslated sources yourself. (b) The KJV translation—which might mean (although not necessarily) that you are
interested in the Bible's literary reception history. (c) A more
accessible contemporary English translation. (d) Something else.

3   What literary works can you think of that sound like the Bible
in some way? What effect does this create for you when you
read such a work?

4   The Bible has been listened to at least as often as it has been read
in silence. Do you prefer to hear the Bible read aloud or to read
the words silently? Why?

SUGGESTIONS FOR FURTHER READING

Consider reading one or more of the literary and biblical texts mentioned above. An excellent scholarly edition of the KJV is the two-
volume Norton Critical Edition edited by Herbert Marks (the Old

Testament) and Gerald Hammond and Austin Busch (the New Testament and Apocrypha). These volumes include not only insightful notes but also excerpts of relevant secondary works, London: W. W. Norton, 2012.

For translations of Hebrew scripture that help illuminate the ancient features of the texts sometimes lost in other translations, see Robert Alter's *The Five Books of Moses*, New York: W. W. Norton, 2004, *Ancient Israel: The Former Prophets*, New York: W. W. Norton, 2013, *The Wisdom Books*, New York: W. W. Norton, 2010, and *The Book of Psalms*, New York: W. W. Norton, 2007; see also Everett Fox's *The Five Books of Moses*, New York: Schocken, 2000 and *The Early Prophets*, New York: Schocken, 2014.

For relevant secondary works, consider the following:

Daniell, David. *The Bible in English: Its History and Influence.* New Haven: Yale University Press, 2003. Daniell offers a detailed account of the history of English Bible translations. See also Gerald Hammond, *The Making of the English Bible*. Manchester: Carcanet New Press, 1982 and Alister McGrath, *In the Beginning: The Story of the King James Bible and How It Changed a Nation, a Language, and a Culture*. New York: Random House, 2001.

Hamlin, Hannibal, and Norman W. Jones, eds. *The King James Bible after 400 Years: Literary, Linguistic, and Cultural Influences.* Cambridge: Cambridge University Press, 2010. This collection explores the literary and cultural legacy of the KJV from a variety of angles; see especially essays by Stephen Pricket, Paul C. Gutjahr, James Wood, and Norman W. Jones. See also Robert Alter, *Pen of Iron: American Prose and the King James Bible*. Princeton: Princeton University Press, 2010 and Shirley A. Stave, ed., *Toni Morrison and the Bible: Contested Intertextualities*. New York: Peter Lang, 2006.

Kirby-Smith, H. T. *The Origins of Free Verse*. Ann Arbor: University of Michigan Press, 1996. This study describes Whitman's poetry as "biblical-anaphoric free verse," drawing on the rhetorical figure, anaphora (the repetition of initial words or phrases), to characterize the cumulative enumeration inspired by biblical uses of repetition and parallelism.

Pelikan, Jaroslav. *Who Bible Is It? A History of the Scriptures through the Ages*. New York: Penguin, 2005. Pelikan offers a readable and scholarly history of the Bible.

CONCLUSION: A SECULAR AGE?

For more than a thousand years the Bible has exerted tremendous influence on Anglophone imaginative literatures. Yet what of the future? We live in a pluralistic age in the sense that different worldviews—both religious and secular—exist in close proximity with one another. These view are often in tension, to say the least. Some scholars therefore describe the twenty-first century as a "secular age" inasmuch as many people have a sense that any worldview is just one of many possibilities. Certainly, the Bible cannot be said to possess the same kind of widespread authority that it once possessed in most English-speaking cultures. Is the Bible's literary influence waning?

To help answer that question, consider again the larger story told in the preceding chapters. First, when we interpret the Bible—whether for sacred or secular purposes—we must use literary methods of reading simply because the Bible so frequently uses literary techniques. Second, the Bible regularly depicts stories as tools for self-reflection. Taken together, these two claims help explain why the Bible has such a special relationship with imaginative literature, whether through direct allusions, specific forms of resonance, or broad cultural trends in literary history. Indeed, the modern notion of "the literary" is deeply intertwined with and partly derives from the Bible's reception history.

The literary nature of the Bible is especially evident in its use of figurative representations to convey its own limitations: on various levels, it seems to tell a tale that cannot be fully or clearly told. One of the profoundest tensions in the Bible derives from its depictions of God as transcendent yet also immanent—beyond human understanding yet capable of being at least partially known through scripture as well as through intimate human relationships. Such relationships seem to attest to divine transcendence in certain biblical stories even while many other biblical stories emphasize the suffering created when such relationships get broken by betrayal or rejection.

Another aspect of the transcendence-versus-immanence tension concerns the justice of God. Are God's punishments and rewards immediate, deferred, or somehow beyond conventional human understandings of justice? Does the Bible present a coherent sense of justice at all? To what extent do human characters in the Bible seem responsible for their actions? Monster stories constitute one of the most popular literary ways of exploring these and related questions. A broader array of stories involving unlikely heroes and unexpected kinds of heroism often draw on the Bible's subversion of insider-versus-outsider hierarchies. The Bible's thematic concerns for the outcast and oppressed as well as its complex history of being invoked on behalf of the powerful as well as the powerless—both the centers and margins of society—make it an especially rich intertext for modern and contemporary literary representations of marginalized voices.

Turning to formal characteristics of the Bible, the distinctive "sound" of the Authorized or King James Version (KJV) derives from such a variety of formal features that components of it can be heard in writing styles as different as those of William Wordsworth, Gerard Manley Hopkins, William Faulkner, and Ernest Hemingway. The KJV has influenced the history of free verse, especially through the poetry of Walt Whitman. In some twentieth- and twenty-first century narratives, the KJV sound may be heard as a kind of ghostly voice.

Some might object that, in providing a comprehensive overview of the Bible in terms of its literary legacy, I have overemphasized traditional religious interpretations of the Bible that assume it functions as a unified whole. Yet such interpretations constitute a highly influential aspect of its literary reception history. They therefore help us better understand that history. They also help us better understand the tensions and questions that have arisen alongside and sometimes within traditional religious interpretations.

Others might accuse me of overemphasizing interpretive tensions in the Bible. Yet it is important to remember that this book focuses on the Bible's *literary* reception history: these tensions deeply inform that history. Mikhail Bakhtin argued that the Bible is so authoritative that it does not allow what he called *multivocality*, a term he used to describe the ability for a novel to "speak" in different "voices"—to represent different perspectives in tension with one another without subsuming or otherwise unifying them into one dominant perspective. The extraordinarily diverse variety of imaginative literature influenced by the Bible tells a different story from Bakhtin's, bearing witness to a long tradition of interpretations that wrestle with the tensions described in this book. Indeed, these tensions are key to understanding the literary legacy of the Bible. Many of the most interesting literary works influenced by the Bible tend not to forward one solution to such tensions but instead wrestle with and creatively reinterpret the tensions themselves.

When it comes to predicting the future of the Bible's literary influence, these tensions are also key. Declining biblical literacy in general coupled with the declining popularity specifically of the KJV mean that distinctive phrases and formal features of the KJV are less likely than they once were to be recognized by readers or even used by authors today. Instead, biblical themes, imagery, characters, and plots play a stronger and more recognizable role in contemporary literature than the Bible's formal influences do. This is one of the reasons why this book foregrounds major themes and stories more than formal aspects of the Bible. The biblical themes described in this book—especially the tensions within them—continue to fascinate both readers and authors alike.

All indications suggest that they will continue to do so, despite that the Bible is a religious text in what many people would describe as "a secular age." In recent years, scholars have shown the term *secular* to be more complicated than was once assumed. A common modern definition of *secular* means *non-religious* (the definition used throughout this book). An older definition referred to aspects of Christian societies (such as England in the seventeenth century) that were the purview of state government rather than the church.

Philosopher Charles Taylor proposes a third definition whereby *secular* refers to contemporary contexts in which religious belief is seen as eminently contestable, just one optional worldview among many.

In part, Taylor aims to help correct the oversimplified secularization narrative that has long dominated modern Western scholarship—a narrative that casts Western modernity as increasingly non-religious and that assumes a secular-versus-religious dichotomy that associates the former with rationality and the latter with superstition. Recent scholarship shows that this dichotomy or binary is not as fixed or definite as it might sometimes seem. This is not to say that there is no difference between secular and religious worldviews but rather that definitions of *secular* and *religious* (and *spiritual*, too) have changed quite a bit, historically. Their meanings depend on specific contexts and points of view. In our ever-shrinking world, it is clear that not everyone defines these terms the same way. Indeed, some do not see hard-and-fast distinctions between the secular and the religious, as is evident in many important works of contemporary literature.

Indeed, as scholars have become more willing in recent years to pay attention to religious intertexts and themes in imaginative literatures, we seem to be realizing that these themes and intertexts never really left us but have been part of our literary traditions all along. Recent work by scholars such as Amy Hungerford and John A. McClure, for example, shows that religious tensions and speculations lie at the heart of much of the most widely respected imaginative literature produced over the past half century—works by Thomas Pynchon, Don DeLillo, Cormac McCarthy, and David Foster Wallace, in addition to the many contemporary authors discussed in this book.

Some of these works may be described as *postsecular* because they represent religious themes as significant elements of their fictional worlds that are neither rejected nor fully embraced (at least not in traditional ways). Many postsecular works implicitly question the ostensible naturalness or inevitability of the secular-religious binary. They thereby nudge readers to think about other ways of understanding that binary—and sometimes other ways of understanding the socioeconomic divisions and hierarchies informed by terms such as "religious" and "secular."

In this aspect of contemporary literature, as well as in the many other aspects of literary history surveyed in this book—from *Beowulf* to *The Book of Salt*—the Bible has played and continues to play a vital role in Anglophone literary traditions.

SUGGESTIONS FOR FURTHER READING

If you want just one book that provides a wide historical range of biblically inspired literary works (including contemporary ones), see Robert Atwan and Laurance Wieder's *Chapters into Verse: A Selection of Poetry in English Inspired by the Bible from Genesis through Revelation*, Oxford: Oxford University Press, 2000. (There is also a two-volume 1993 edition.) For such an anthology that includes not only poetry but also prose fiction excerpts (as well as useful secondary readings), see David Jasper and Stephen Prickett's *The Bible and Literature: A Reader*, Oxford: Blackwell, 1999.

Scholarly works referred to in this chapter include Mikhail Bakhtin's *The Dialogic Imagination: Four Essays*, Carol Emerson and Michael Holquist, trans., Austin: University of Texas Press, 2004; Amy Hungerford's *Postmodern Belief: American Literature and Religion since 1960*, Princeton: Princeton University Press, 2010; and John A. McClure's *Partial Faiths: Postsecular Fiction in the Age of Pynchon and Morrison*, Athens: University of Georgia Press, 2007.

For additional scholarly work in secularization theory, see Talal Asad's *Formations of the Secular: Christianity, Islam, Modernity*, Stanford: Stanford University Press, 2003.; Charles Taylor's *A Secular Age*, Cambridge, MA: The Belknap Press, 2007; and Manav Ratti's *The Postsecular Imagination: Postcolonialism, Religion, and Literature*, Abingdon: Routledge, 2014.

A NOTE ON ENGLISH BIBLE TRANSLATIONS

The 1611 Authorized or King James Version (KJV) has been the most influential English Bible for most of the past four hundred years. (For more about the KJV as well as earlier English translations, see Chapter 5). Dozens of other translations were published before the twentieth century but failed to displace the KJV. Only in the 1980s, by which time several translations produced in the 1950s and 1960s had gained considerable popularity, did a contemporary version finally displace the KJV as the bestselling English Bible.

Today, no single translation dominates English-speaking markets as the KJV once did. Readers may choose from a wealth of options—all the more so since publishers often issue the same translation in different editions with explanatory notes geared toward different audiences (e.g., for women, men, teenagers, etc.). I cannot hope to provide a comprehensive overview of contemporary English translations; instead, I offer the following brief guide to a few representative examples of the most widely used versions.

Readers who feel drawn to the KJV but prefer more contemporary English may find a good compromise in the New King James Version (NKJV). For more thoroughly contemporary versions that regularly echo the KJV, the New Revised Standard Version (NRSV) or the English Standard Version (ESV) are good choices.

The NRSV and ESV are revisions of the 1952 Revised Standard Version (RSV). The NRSV does not harmonize the Old and New Testaments in passages such as Isaiah 7:14 (traditionally read by Christians as foretelling the birth of Jesus) whereas the ESV does. The NRSV uses gender-inclusive language whereas the ESV does not (e.g., Genesis 1:27).

Additional popular translations include the New International Version (NIV) and the New Jerusalem Bible (NJB). The NJB is a Catholic translation; the NIV is a favorite among Evangelical Christians. The NIV harmonizes the Old and New Testaments in passages such as Isaiah 7:14 whereas the NJB does not. The 2011 version of the NIV sometimes uses gender-inclusive language (e.g., in 1 John 4:20–1 and Revelation 3:20 but not in Genesis 1:27), whereas the NJB does so even less frequently (e.g., only in Revelation 3:20 of the three passages previously noted).

To some ears, the most contemporary sounding translations are those that favor "dynamic equivalence" (thought-for-thought) strategies more than "formal equivalence" (word-for-word) ones (it is worth noting that the distinction between the two is not always clear-cut). Among these, the New Living Translation (NLT) is especially popular.

Having so many Bible translations to choose from can help illuminate the complexities of the original sources. It can be well worth your time to go to a local bookstore or library to compare different versions—or use a website that allows you to compare side-by-side translations of the same passage, such as Biblegateway.com or Biblehub.com (see below for more information about online resources).

ONLINE RESOURCES

Many Bible-study resources (online as well as in printed form) are created and maintained by religiously affiliated groups. While it is worth keeping this in mind, even readers who do not share such religious affiliations will find many of these resources to be quite useful. The following are just a few of the many resources available online.

Bible Gateway and Bible Hub are two different Christian websites that offer a wide variety of searchable Bible translations: <https://www.biblegateway.com/> and <http://biblehub.com/>

The Catholic Encyclopedia provides a wealth of information relating to the Bible (and Christianity more broadly) from a Catholic perspective: <http://www.catholic.org/encyclopedia/>

The Encyclopedia Judaica offers illuminating explanations of Hebrew scripture as well as Jewish culture and history: <http://www.bjeindy.org/resources/library/encyclopediajudaica/>

The Oxford Companion to the Bible is a comprehensive scholarly reference source with no religious affiliation: <http://www.oxfordreference.com/view/10.1093/acref/9780195046458.001.0001/acref-9780195046458>

ADDITIONAL SECONDARY SOURCES

It would require an additional book to provide a comprehensive bibliography of the vast scholarship that addresses the relationship between the Bible and literature. This book aims instead to offer guided points of entry into this larger body of scholarship through the suggestions for further reading at the end of each chapter. The following list offers a few additional points of entry into that scholarship. This list focuses on books, but a wealth of relevant articles are also available: simply enter "the Bible and literature" or "the Bible and [the author or title of a literary work]" as your search terms in an online database or search engine, or browse journals such as *Christianity and Literature* and *Religion and Theology*.

Alter, Robert. *Canon and Creativity: Modern Writing and the Authority of Scripture*. New Haven: Yale University Press, 2000.

Berkner, Will. *The Great Mural: The World of Biblical Novels*. Lima, OH: Fairway Press, 1994.

Boitani, Piero. *The Bible and Its Rewritings*. Oxford and New York: Oxford University Press, 1999.

Crain, Jeanie C. *Reading the Bible as Literature*. Cambridge: Polity, 2010.

Dempsey, Carol J. and Elizabeth Michael Boyle. *The Bible and Literature*. New York: Orbis, 2015.

Fairman, Marion. *Biblical Patterns in Modern Literature*. Cleveland: Dillon/Liederbach, 1972.

Fisch, Harold. *The Biblical Presence in Shakespeare, Milton, and Blake: A Comparative Study*. Oxford: Clarendon Press; New York: Oxford University Press, 1999.

—— *New Stories for Old: Biblical Patterns in the Novel*. Basingstoke: Macmillan Press; New York: St. Martin's Press, 1998.

Frye, Northrop. *The Great Code: The Bible and Literature*. New York: Mariner, 2002.

Henderson, Heather. *The Victorian Self: Autobiography and Biblical Narrative*. Ithaca: Cornell University Press, 1989.

Hirsch, David H. and Nehama Aschkenasy, eds. *Biblical Patterns in Modern Literature*. Chico, CA: Scholars Press, 1984.

Jasper, David. *Readings in the Canon of Scripture: Written for Our Learning*. New York: St. Martin's Press, 1995.

Knight, Mark, ed. *Biblical Religion and the Novel, 1700–2000*. Aldershot and Burlington, VT: Ashgate, 2006.

Lemon, Rebecca, Emma Mason, Jonathan Roberts, and Christopher Rowland, eds. *The Blackwell Companion to the Bible in English Literature*. Chichester: Wiley-Blackwell, 2009.

Stahlberg, Lesleigh Cushing. *Sustaining Fictions: Intertextuality, Midrash, Translation, and the Literary Afterlife of the Bible*. New York: T & T Clark, 2008.

Swindell, Anthony C. *Reworking the Bible: The Literary Reception-History of Fourteen Biblical Stories*. Sheffield: Sheffield Phoenix, 2010.

Tichy, H. J. *Biblical Influences in English Literature: A Survey of Studies*. Ann Arbor: Edwards Bros., 1953.

Vance, Norman. *Bible and Novel: Narrative Authority and the Death of God*. Oxford: Oxford University Press, 2013.

Zemka, Sue. *Victorian Testaments: The Bible, Christology, and Literary Authority in Early-Nineteenth-Century British Culture*. Stanford: Stanford University Press, 1997.

INDEX